MW01671503

Infant/Toddler Sensory Profile™

User's Manual

Winnie Dunn, Ph.D., OTR, FAOTA

PEARSON

License to Use

You understand that You have purchased a nonexclusive, nontransferable, revocable, limited License to use the Copyrighted Material pursuant to this limited License. The purchase of this limited License in no way transfers copyrights or other ownership interests to You. You agree that You will not (and shall not permit others to) sublicense, rent, lend, transfer, lease, sell, or provide to others the Copyrighted Material. Permission is hereby granted to You to share or lend the Copyrighted Material only with another professional who meets the Publisher's qualifications for License purchase, as long as such loan or sharing does not otherwise violate this limited license.

Reproducing Pages From This Book

As described below, some of the pages in this book may be reproduced for instructional use (not for resale). To protect your book, make a photocopy of each reproducible page. Then use that copy as a master for photocopying.

Portions of this work were published in previous editions.

Figure 2.1 adapted and reprinted with permission from Aspen Publishers.

Published by Pearson
P.O. Box 599700
San Antonio, TX 78259

800.211.8378

www.PsychCorp.com

0761649557

PEARSON

to

Fish Man

[Andrew Timothy Wilson]

who adores me with such intensity

that it takes my breath away…

and makes it possible for me to both persist and flourish

at being myself…

About the Author

Winnie Dunn is professor and chair of the Occupational Therapy Department at the University of Kansas Medical Center. She is author of the *Sensory Profile,* which preceded the *Infant/Toddler Sensory Profile,* in 1999. Dr. Dunn is a Fellow of AOTA and a member of the American Occupational Therapy Foundation's Academy of Research. She also has earned the AOTA's Award of Merit and has received AOTA's Service Award several times.

Most recently Dr. Dunn was appointed the Eleanor Clarke Slagle lecturer (2001), the top academic honor in occupational therapy. Her lecture, entitled *The sensations of everyday life: Empirical, theoretical, and pragmatic considerations,* included reflections on the meaning of her work on all the *Sensory Profile* measures. It is published in the December 2001 edition of the *American Journal of Occupational Therapy.*

She earned a B.S. in Occupational Therapy and an M.S. in Education/Learning Disabilities at the University of Missouri at Columbia. She earned a doctorate in Special Studies at the University of Kansas at Lawrence. Additionally, Dr. Dunn has published extensively, authoring or co-authoring more than 80 journal articles, monographs, books, book chapters, and book reviews. She also has served on the editorial boards of *Physical and Occupational Therapy in Pediatrics, Cognitive Rehabilitation,* and the *Occupational Therapy Journal of Research.* She has presented hundreds of papers and workshops during her career.

Contents

Chapter 6

List of Figures

List of Tables

Preface

How could I immerse myself in cooking all these years and never realize that the spices are alphabetized at the grocery store?

I really like cooking. I like thinking about cooking as I read recipes, cookbooks, and magazines. I like the rituals of cooking: grocery shopping, measuring, stirring, chopping, and scheduling how everything will be ready at the same time. I like smelling the items when they are raw and while they are cooking. My family will tell you I like tasting things along the way; this communication might end with "That's disgusting, mom." And I really like arranging the food on the plate and at the table to make a dramatic presentation when it's time to eat.

And to make matters worse, I have poor figure ground perception, so all that scanning to find the spices for all those years was laborious (and no, it did not improve my figure ground perception skills).

So how can a person so interested in a topic remain so oblivious to a factoid like 'the spices are alphabetized?' I know other factoids that are less useful, like 'look for the pine nuts in the ethnic food section, and remember they are called pignoli' (I guess that's 2 factoids). I am much less in need of pine nuts than spices.

I have to admit that there is a pattern to this slow awakening of my awareness. My yoga teacher provides guidance for improving one of my poses, like 'rotate your thigh outward.' She gives me many variations of this guidance, and I even think that I AM rotating my thigh... and then one day I really *do* rotate my thigh, and my consciousness shouts 'oh, *this* is what she meant!' From that moment on, it seems so obvious, and yet it was so elusive prior to that moment.

And lest you believe that this is only a feature of my cognitive performance in personal life, don't be too hasty. I remember (whew, at least I can still do *that*) hearing Jean Ayres speak in Ohio during the formative period of sensory integration knowledge development and thinking '*Wow*, she is giving us some *great* new ideas!' (she always did, by the way), only to return home and discover that she had already presented these ideas several years before in her classic book *Sensory Integration and Learning Disorders*. Although I had read this more than once I did consider the possibility that someone had snuck the new material into my copy while I was gone. Dr. Ayres was always wise, and apparently she knew that some of us had a slow learning curve.

So, why am I telling you these stories that shed a less than stellar light on my performance? I think that sometimes when people pick up a finished work, there is some mystique suggesting that the work just materialized in that form, with all the insights and (hopefully) wisdom intact. The truth is that academic endeavors are no different from any other activities of our lives.

Sometimes we just have to wait until we are ready to know something. We remain present with whatever is interesting to us, keep placing ourselves in the path of knowledge and insight, and trust that wisdom will wash over us in its time. That's the rub; we want to select the time and we don't get to. We can only try to create enough quiet to hear the wisdom when it walks by.

When I worked on the *Sensory Profile,* I was focused on providing a useful tool to operationalize a critical aspect of occupational therapy wisdom so we would have a way to communicate our perspectives about the impact of sensory processing on performance to families and our interdisciplinary colleagues.

It was a great idea, and I think that it is working. My youngest daughter is in graduate school in elementary and special education. A guest lecturer came to one of her classes to talk about strategies for children who have Asperger's syndrome. During the lecture this special educator was listing the characteristics of these children that might interfere with their learning, and then giving the students strategies for teaching these children successfully. My daughter and her peers heard the teacher state that sensory processing differences frequently interfere, and they began looking at each other in that knowing way that occurs when you have figured out what is going to happen next in the story. The teacher did not disappoint them...she talked about this cool test developed by occupational therapists to evaluate sensory processing, and then told the students that occupational therapists have many ideas for helping with these types of problems. What the teacher did not know was that *this* group of students already knew about sensory processing from one of their cohort's mothers.

Am I delighted that our discipline is becoming part of routine conversation in another discipline? *Certainly*. Did I plan this? *Certainly not*.

I had no idea that there would be work past development and study of the application of the *Sensory Profile*. I could no more know this than I could know that the spices are alphabetized or what rotating my thigh meant until it was time to know these things. It was only in completing the *Sensory Profile* and then standing in place to receive the feedback from my interdisciplinary colleagues and families that I began to understand the meaning of that work: to begin to understand the nature of sensory processing. I did not develop the model of sensory processing we are currently working from until *after* the *Sensory Profile* was completed. Once we had some overarching ideas in mind, then it became obvious that we needed to test these ideas across the life span. My colleagues helped me to understand this by clamoring for an Infant/Toddler version and for an Adolescent/Adult version of the *Sensory Profile*.

The truths about sensory processing have always been available to us; by persisting in our interest in sensory processing, our discipine is discovering these truths in service to interdisciplinary knowledge development and better intervention practices.

So, the *Infant/Toddler Sensory Profile* benefits from the clouds clearing about what I was doing in the first place. The items on this version more clearly reflect the constructs in Dunn's Model of Sensory Processing because I knew what they were by this time. This wisdom provides us with a clearer way to characterize young children's sensory processing status and ultimately to understand the contribution of sensory processing to the experience of living.

It is very seductive for me to think that *now* I get it. But I thought I got it before...and I could still cook even though it took me a while to find the spices. I guess the best I can do is recognize that we are as far as we can be for now. Collectively we will be able to use this material in service to the *next* insight.

And as much as we might want to 'get there' faster (wherever 'there' is), it would be like rushing out to eat a persimmon before it is ripe (arghhh!) or bread before it is fully baked...it's unpleasant and you miss the good experience of watching the persimmon ripen through all its beautiful colors or feeling the dough and smelling the bread as it bakes. In fact, you might decide that you don't like persimmons or home baked bread, and remove them from your path, not only missing the journey of discovery but also creating the impoverished path that does not contain the mature form at all.

So I can select my spices alphabetically, I have my thigh rotated outward, who knows what's next? All I can tell you is that I will be standing in place waiting for wisdom to walk by so I can invite her in.

winnie

Acknowledgments

It is certainly an illusion that the person whose name is on the front of a work is the person who produced the material within. Fortunately we have a tradition of shattering this illusion, and we call this process THE ACKNOWLEDGEMENTS.

I am extremely grateful to the many persons who made it possible for me to complete this project. My staff at the University of Kansas provides a constant infrastructure enabling me to be productive each day. Jeannie Rigby, Bonnie Danley, Carol Hydeman, and Lynn Hurd tirelessly support my intense professional life and I thank them for this commitment to our department and to me.

I also acknowledge my colleague and doctoral student **Deb Daniels, M.A., CCC**, who worked with me to identify and edit test items throughout the developmental process. We share a philosophy of interdisciplinary collaboration and family-centered care, and these ideas are reflected in this tool.

I am also grateful to the graduate students and faculty at the University of Kansas for their various contributions to item development, organization, analysis and interpretation in the evolution of the *Infant/Toddler Sensory Profile.*

What can I say about **Jessi Saiter, OTR**? She is a tenacious, enthusiastic and open-hearted therapist who is completely dedicated to our profession and the families she serves. I have had the complete fortune of having her as my Research Assistant during this process. I have come to rely on her completely when we have had deadlines, when we have had to return to the original data sets to confirm our findings, and when we have had to make difficult decisions about which scores would be most helpful for our colleagues in practice. Her spirit is woven through this material, and I know that each of the readers will notice and feel her energy along with mine.

I also thank those at The Psychological Corporation for their commitment to the *Sensory Profile* projects. Of particular note is my dear colleague Gay Lynn Lamey, Project Director, who has come to know my words so well, she can tell when someone else has drafted a sentence! She loves this project, and recognizes the gift it is to our profession, and to the children and families we serve. I am also grateful to Margaret Young Cooley, Editor; Dr. Charles "Chuck" Wilkins, Psychometrician Team Manager; Dr. Larry Price, Psychometrician; Marian Zahora, Designer; and Mark W. Cooley, Production Coordinator, for adding their expertise to improving the product.

Families are the central factor in my ability to complete this project. Although I do not know each of their names, I am eternally grateful to them for trusting the professionals in their lives to use their family's perspectives in a safe way that helps everyone. Without this trust, we would have no data, and therefore no information to share.

Colleagues responded to my request to provide data from families across the nation. Additionally, students in professional and graduate programs in occupational therapy and speech pathology made contributions to data collection, data entry and idea generation as part of their education programs. These individuals are the only reason that I am able to create materials like the *Infant/Toddler Sensory Profile* for our professional work.

Lynne M. Adams
Maggie Altom
Michelle Anderson
Rebecca L. Atencio
Mille Atz
Margaret Bachman
Nichole Bailey
Cary Ballesteros
Sarah Banker
Laura A. Barbin
Brandi Beatson
Susie Beiler
Marianne Belcke
Jana Bennett
Dee Berline
Jeff Bezzant
Joan Bishop
Bonnie Bobet-Beyhl
Martha Boye
Angela D. Brouhard
Amber H. Brown
Lauren Brown
George D. Burright
Richard Buvey
Nancy Carbia
Nancy Carlino
Tracy Chambers
Gayle Chaney
Taira Christiansen
Jenny Clark
Cindy Clark
Tina Marie Collop
Tonia Cook-Gardner
Barbara Cracchiolo
Patty Cunningham
Cindy D'Alberto
Mariana D'Amico
Tiffany Daley
Bonnie Danley
Loan Dao
Donita Davis
Janice Deetscreek
Cathy Deitch
Joan Delahunt
Catherine DeLeon
Diane Demaio-Feldman
Susann DeTienne
Rachel B. Diamant
Joann Distefano
Wilma Dorman
Mary Dueker
Dana Dunbar
Paticia Eggleston
Norma Eigles
Amy Eisele
Amber Leigh Ellis
Kathleen Engebretson
Rita Esposito
Bonnie L. Fellows
Sally Fennema-Jansen
Marijana Filomarino
Michelle Fisher
Ella Fitzmayer
Stephanie Foster
Carole Ann Fournier
Doreen Fraits-Hunt
Kristin Frerichs Murphy
Karen Fried
Gloria Frolek Clark
Mary-Ann Fulks
Roena Gabbard
Vera Gallagher
Dawn Garfield-Blades
Debbie Gauthreaux
Bethnay Gerther-Kent
Vera Goodman
Irene Gordon
Natalie Gorlin
Mary Grassi
Monica Green
Maryn Green
Susan Guertin
Tracy Gunderman
Debra K. Hamilton
Margaret Hare
Rita Anne Haskins
Roseann Hatchett
Annette Hatter
Melanie Heffley
Alisa Henry
Julie Marie Herbert
Susan Hochhalter
Catherine Hostetler
Ellen Hughson-Hale
Shelby Ivory
Becky Jardine
Alba Jirau
Ketti Johnson-Coffelt
Renee Johnson-Shelley
Kristi Kersten
Mary Kientz
Kelly Kleinhaus
Karen J. Knight
Larry Ladd
Gay Lamey
Robin Lang
MaryJo Laughlin
Michelle Leeker
Lauri Levenburg
Diane Lewis
Krisanne Lewis
Jennie Lie
Wendy Robins
Lisa S. Lipshez
Rebecca Livingstone
Susan Lizotte
Lea Manny
Jacqueline Mast
Sue McAllister
Helga Medican
Terri Meier
Ellen Mellard
Dulce M. Mendoza
Rose Mary Merola
Kristie Middendorf
Kathryn Miesner
Nancy Miller
Nancy Mooers
Ruth T. Morales
Sharon Motechin
Kelly Mullin
Dean L. Murray
Joan Mutchler
Charolette Myles-Nixon
Phyllis Nayak
Barbara Ness
Ariela Neuman
Patricia Neville

Lisa Nguyen-Dao
Becky Nicholson
Matt Nielson
Susan M. Nieman
Becky Nies
Carmen L. Nodsle
Therese Nugent
Kathleen O'Grady Graham
Jaimev Orne Owings
Marjorie Paller
Christine Parks
Elba I. Perez Rios
Roger D. Phillips
Therese Place
Carol Pociecha-Palm
Laura Poliquin
Jennifer L. Potter
Marcia Pressler
Maryann Radowski
Cynthia Radue
Damarys I. Ruiz Ramos
Cynthia Randall
Sara Rasmussen
Carol Richardson
E. Judith Riggin
Lou Rinner
Dawn Rottinghaus
Marilyn Runyon
Kristin D. Saccento
Jessi Saiter
Barbara Sarbaugh
Al Sarno
Carole Schaffer
Lisa Scheet
Hali Scheiner
Kathryn Schlaudecker
Kathleen C. Schlenz
Jean Schukei
Jodie Seligson
Rebecca Sheehan
Evelyn Ann Sickel
Mergeret Singer
Jada Smith
Nancy H. Smith
Patricia Sperle
Deidre Stewart
Wendy Stewart
Jacqueline Swan
Michele Tagliabue
Tracey Marie Taylor
Carla Tellez
Debra Tipton
Linda Tirella
Katherine Townsend
Janet Tredwell
Laura Trent
Rosalyn Vermeulen
Margaret Rita Visentin
Deborah Vokes
Jill Wegner
Carolyn Wendt
Debra J. Wilhelm
Greg Wills
Teri Wiss
Cheri Wojton
Albert K. S. Wong
Deborah A. Wooldridge
Greg Wootton
Sandra Yasskin
Esther C. Zapata

Students who participated in development of the tool

Jill Arnold
Derri Banman
Brandyn Beatson
Michelle Blankenbaker
Lauren Brown
Heather Buckley
Kristin Campbell
Debbie Daniels
Loan Dao
Carla DeDonder
Joan Delahunt
Loren Dickenson
Melanie Heffley
Beverly Huneck
Casse Jones
Mandi Keddle
Amanda Lukert
Renee Miller
Stacy Pate
Jessi Saiter
Lisa Shallenburger
Marcia Sloan

CHAPTER 1

Overview

The *Infant/Toddler Sensory Profile* provides a standard method for professionals to measure a child's sensory processing abilities and to profile the effect of sensory processing on functional performance in the daily life of a child. This version of the profile is designed for children birth to 3 years of age. The *Infant/Toddler Sensory Profile* was designed to contribute to a comprehensive assessment of a child's performance when combined with other evaluations, observations, and reports, and provides another perspective on the child's strengths and challenges for diagnostic and intervention planning.

The *Infant/Toddler Sensory Profile* is a judgment-based caregiver questionnaire. Each item describes children's responses to various sensory experiences. The caregiver who has daily contact with the child completes the questionnaire by reporting the frequency with which these behaviors occur (Almost Always, Frequently, Occasionally, Seldom, or Almost Never). The therapist or other professional then scores the responses on the questionnaire. Certain patterns of performance on the *Infant/Toddler Sensory Profile* are indicative of difficulties with sensory processing and performance. In these cases, the team serving the child follows up on the relationship between sensory processing and performance difficulties. Occupational therapists have expertise in sensory processing as part of their professional preparation. Other professionals can acquire this expertise through post-professional education.

The *Infant/Toddler Sensory Profile* consists of 36 items for children birth to 6 months and 48 items for children 7 to 36 months, and the questionnaire is available both in English and Spanish. The caregiver questionnaire contains items divided into sensory systems. For children birth to 6 months, there are four quadrant scores and one combined quadrant score; for children 7 to 36 months, there are five sensory processing section scores, four quadrant scores, and one combined quadrant score available.

The quadrant scores reflect the child's responsiveness to sensory experiences, and are based on Dunn's Model of Sensory Processing (see Chapter 2). Sensation Seeking and Low Registration indicate different high threshold responses, while Sensory Sensitivity and Sensation Avoiding reflect different low threshold responses. Because the low threshold items are particularly relevant with some disability groups, we also provide a combined quadrant score (Low Threshold) that is the combination of Sensory Sensitivity and Sensation Avoiding quadrant scores.

The Sensory Processing scores for children 7 to 36 months indicate the child's responses to the basic sensory systems. Although there are six sensory processing systems addressed in the questionnaire (i.e., General Processing, Auditory Processing, Visual Processing, Tactile Processing, Vestibular Processing, and Oral Sensory Processing), only five sensory processing systems for children 7 to 36 months have scores: Auditory Processing, Visual Processing, Tactile Processing, Vestibular Processing and Oral Sensory Processing. The General Processing items did not meet acceptable levels of reliability and therefore were not used as a score.

Purpose

The *Infant/Toddler Sensory Profile* is a tool for linking performance strengths and barriers with the child's sensory processing patterns. Its purpose is to evaluate the possible contributions of sensory processing to the child's daily performance patterns and to provide information about his or her tendencies to respond to stimuli and which sensory systems are likely to be contributing to or creating barriers to functional performance.

Rationale

When a child is referred for an evaluation, the members of the interdisciplinary team bring unique frames of reference to the assessment process, including different ways of interpreting the same behavior. Regardless of the frame of reference a professional uses, each team member has the responsibility to develop hypotheses that link the child's abilities to the child's performance. Some assessment methods yield good diagnostic information but do not provide clear links to performance; other assessment methods enable professionals to verify performance problems, but provide no mechanism for linking this information to frames of reference for theory-based decision making.

The *Infant/Toddler Sensory Profile* uses a sensory processing and neuroscience frame of reference and supports a family-centered care philosophy by involving the caregivers in the data-gathering process. The *Infant/Toddler Sensory Profile* facilitates decision making by providing the necessary link between performance in daily life and theory.

Benefits

Following are benefits to the caregiver and professional using the *Infant/Toddler Sensory Profile*.

1. The *Infant/Toddler Sensory Profile* provides a natural way to include families in the information-gathering process. Caregivers complete the profile, reporting their own experiences with their child. Evaluation tools that solicit the caregivers' expertise support family-centered care models of practice.
2. Caregivers report a therapeutic benefit from completing the *Infant/Toddler Sensory Profile*. The items are familiar to caregivers living with infants and toddlers who have sensory processing problems. Reading about their child's "idiosyncratic" behaviors during assessment provides validation that there is something real about their family's experience and suggests that there may be some ways to deal with it.

3. The *Infant/Toddler Sensory Profile* provides professionals with a way to capture the child's responses during the natural course of daily life, a task difficult or impossible to achieve with formal evaluations in unfamiliar settings. For all professionals, a child's functional performance in daily life must be a central focus. Because there are few evaluation tools that measure performance in daily life, the *Infant/Toddler Sensory Profile* is a viable option.
4. The *Infant/Toddler Sensory Profile* is constructed so that professionals can engage in theory-based decision making during comprehensive assessment and intervention planning. Principles of neuroscience, sensory processing, and occupational performance are embedded in the items and scoring structure. By following the guidelines for use in this manual, professionals can make decisions that are consistent with these theoretical principles.
5. The *Infant/Toddler Sensory Profile* provides both a measure of current performance and an indication of intervention directions. Test results provide information about the child's level of responsivity to sensory events (e.g., hyperresponsive or hyporesponsive). Because the *Infant/Toddler Sensory Profile* is organized into sections, test results also suggest which sensory systems might be interfering with the child's performance and which daily life tasks might be more difficult. The information gained from the *Infant/Toddler Sensory Profile* provides status measurement of current performance levels; the scoring structure of the *Infant/Toddler Sensory Profile* provides guideposts for planning interventions with the families and other caregivers.

Goals and Features

A primary goal of the *Infant/Toddler Sensory Profile* research process was to develop an evaluation tool that enables professionals to gather information about the child's sensory processing abilities, and how those patterns support and/or interfere with functional performance. Another goal was extension of the age range of the *Sensory Profile* measure, used for preschool and school-age children. The *Infant/Toddler Sensory Profile*:

1. captures salient information about infants' and toddlers' sensory processing;
2. clearly links sensory processing with the child's daily life performance;
3. provides information for theory-based decision making;
4. includes caregivers as critical members of the team;
5. is applicable for young children with all types of disabilities and severity levels;
6. is easy to administer, score, and interpret; and
7. is quick to administer.

Test Components

The *Infant/Toddler Sensory Profile* consists of a *User's Manual*, a combined *Caregiver Questionnaire* for children ages birth to 6 months and children ages 7 to 36 months, and a combined *Summary Score Sheet* for children ages birth to 6 months and children ages 7 to 36 months.

User's Manual

The *User's Manual* contains information about the rationale, theory, and development of the *Infant/Toddler Sensory Profile* and specific information about the administration, scoring, and interpretation of the scores. The manual also contains case studies and intervention suggestions.

Caregiver Questionnaire

The *Caregiver Questionnaire* contains 36 items for children ages birth to 6 months starting on the front of the questionnaire and 48 items for children ages 7 to 36 months reversed and starting on the back of the questionnaire. These items describe children's responses to daily sensory experiences. Caregivers complete the form by indicating the frequency of the child's responses (Almost Always, Frequently, Occasionally, Seldom, or Almost Never) to various sensory experiences. The *Caregiver Questionnaire* is available in English and Spanish. See page 56 for more information on the research completed with the Spanish version of the *Infant/Toddler Sensory Profile*.

Summary Score Sheet

The *Summary Score Sheet* provides a summary of the child's scores. It is divided into two sections, one for children ages birth to 6 months, and one for children ages 7 to 36 months. The *Summary Score Sheet* contains an area to record demographic information, a Quadrant Grid to help summarize the child's scores in the designated groupings, and a Quadrant Summary to plot raw score totals into performance categories. Included in the section for children ages 7 to 36 months is an added Sensory Processing Section Summary.

Administration Time

Caregivers report that it takes 15 minutes to complete the *Caregiver Questionnaire*. The *Summary Score Sheet* will take the examiner 15 minutes to complete.

User Qualifications

Individuals from many different professions can administer the *Infant/Toddler Sensory Profile*. Both service providers and researchers will find the test results useful. Service providers such as occupational therapists, teachers, psychologists, speech-language pathologists, and physicians might use it to gain a picture of a child's performance during daily life, as well as determine areas of strength and areas of concern that can help provide the foundation for intervention planning. Basic science researchers might include the instrument in their protocols as a functional measure of sensory responsivity. Applied science researchers might use it to gather data linking sensory processing to daily life.

This manual provides a framework for interpreting the caregivers' responses. However, proper interpretation of the child's scores requires some understanding of sensory processing and its impact on performance. The References section contains cited works for additional reading. Professionals who are new to considering the sensory processing aspects of children's performance should consult with an occupational therapist or other professional with a background in sensory processing before including *Infant/Toddler Sensory Profile* interpretations in their reports.

Cut Scores and Classification System

Researchers defined two classification systems, one for children ages birth to 6 months and one for children ages 7 to 36 months, by determining cut scores for each quadrant raw score total and/or sensory processing section.

The classification system for children ages **birth to 6 months** describes the child's sensory processing abilities for each quadrant and a combined quadrant as either:

- Typical Performance or
- Consult and Follow-up.

The classification system for children ages **7 to 36 months** describes the child's sensory processing abilities for each quadrant, a combined quadrant, and sensory processing section as:

- Typical Performance,
- Probable Difference, or
- Definite Difference.

The classification systems help the professional quickly determine whether a child's performance on the *Infant/Toddler Sensory Profile* is of concern. Chapter 3 provides a detailed explanation of the derivation of cut scores and the classification system.

CHAPTER 2

Theoretical and Conceptual Features

Conceptual Model for the *Infant/Toddler Sensory Profile*

The *Infant/Toddler Sensory Profile* characterizes children's behaviors and performance in relation to sensory processing. Research findings with older children led to a conceptual model that hypothesizes an interaction between neurological thresholds and behavioral responses (Dunn, 1997a). The interaction of these two continua provides a method for explaining how children process sensory information and provides guidance for intervention planning. Figure 2.1 on page 8 illustrates the conceptual model and its components.

Neurological threshold refers to the amount of stimuli required for a neuron or neuron system to respond. At one end of this continuum, thresholds are very high; this means it would take a lot of stimuli to meet the threshold and fire the neurons. At the other end of this continuum, thresholds are very low; this means it takes very little stimuli to meet the threshold and fire the neurons.

Behavioral response/self-regulation refers to the way people act in consideration of their thresholds. At one end of this continuum, children respond passively in relation to their thresholds. This means they would have a tendency to let the nervous system respond (or not respond), and they would behave consistently with this neural activity. At the other end of the behavioral continuum, children respond actively in relation to their thresholds. This means they would work against their thresholds as a way to reach homeostasis. You might also consider these responses as the child's self-regulation strategies.

Principles and Features of the Neurological Threshold Continuum

The entire nervous system operates based on excitation and inhibition. Excitation occurs when the neurons are more likely to respond or are activated. Inhibition occurs when the likelihood of responding is decreased or responses are blocked. It is the balance of these operations that determines when responses are generated; some refer to this balance of the neurological continuum as *modulation*. Modulation is the brain's regulation of neural messages by facilitating or inhibiting responses. When modulation is intact, the nervous system responds to some stimuli while ignoring other stimuli, and the child generates an appropriate adaptive response to the situation.

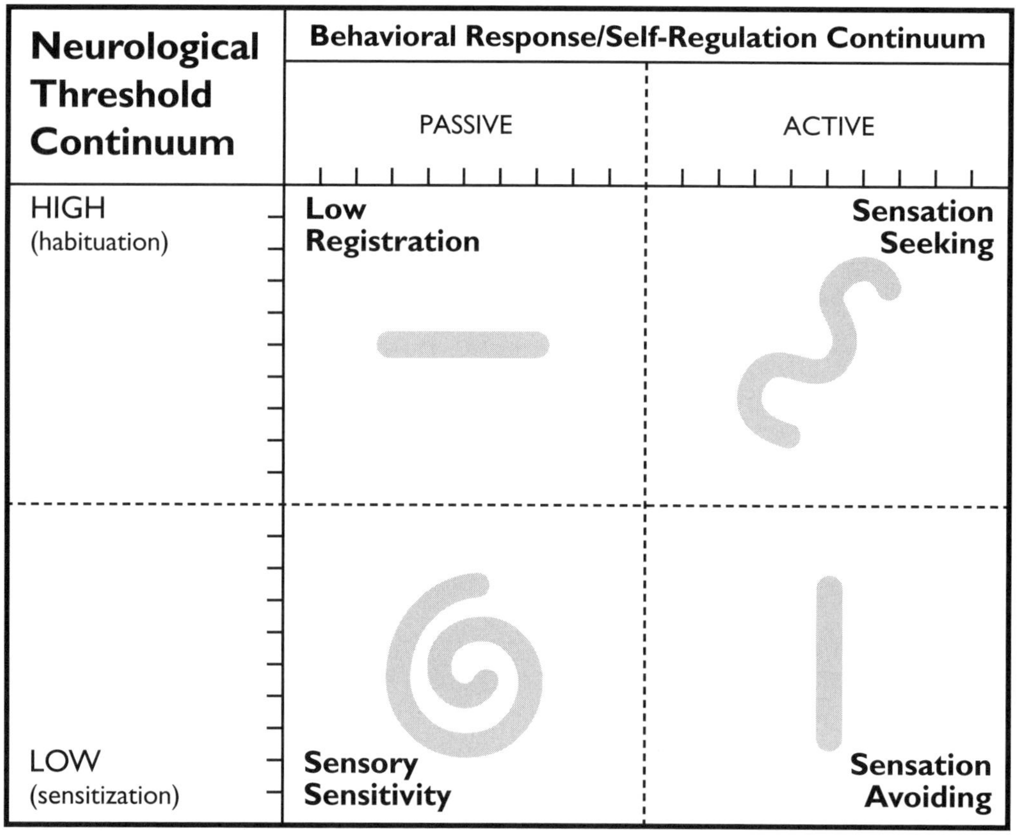

Figure 2.1 ■ **Relationships Between Behavioral Response/Self-Regulation and Neurological Thresholds***

In the neuroscience literature, the extreme ends of the neurological threshold continuum are called *habituation* and *sensitization*. Habituation is a process that represents the nervous system's recognition that something familiar has occurred. At the cellular level, we can say that the neuron has experienced the firing pattern, and after a time, this familiar pattern no longer needs attention. At a system level, children need habituation to cope with the myriad of stimuli available at any moment in their day. Without habituation, children would be distracted continually by each new stimulus, including how their clothing feels, the sounds in the hall, the flowers blowing in the breeze outside the window, the sound and feel of saliva being swallowed, etc. Humans need habituation to focus their attention to tasks at hand. When people have difficulty with habituation, they may appear distracted, agitated, or inattentive. Their nervous systems keep interrupting ongoing performance to notice each new stimulus that comes along.

Sensitization is the nervous system mechanism that enhances potentially important stimuli. Some stimuli require attention right away, although they might be familiar. This is particularly true when the organism anticipates harm or danger associated with the stimulus. Once the nervous system identifies a stimulus as one requiring heightened attention, more neurons can be recruited to make the message more powerful and subsequently generate an immediate and powerful response. For example, although the smell of smoke could be a technically small stimulus in the room after

*Adapted and reprinted with permission from Dunn, W., The impact of sensory processing abilities on the daily lives of young children and their families: A conceptual model. *Infants and Young Children*, 9(4), 23–35, copyright © 1997, Aspen Publishers.

bedtime, this stimulus could trigger sensitization (based on its potential harmfulness), so that the person would arouse (even from sleep) and take immediate action to gather more information and/or get out of harm's way. Children develop and use sensitization through life experiences as they grow up so that they can remain attentive to their surroundings while engaged in play and other learning.

As children grow, their nervous systems are evolving and their experiences are shaping the nervous system's evolution. As part of this process, a balance of habituation and sensitization must develop to support adaptive behavior (i.e., appropriate responses to environmental demands). The point along the neurological continuum that is the most likely to generate a response for a particular child is called that child's *threshold* for that stimulus. There is a range of thresholds that supports adaptive behavior and thresholds that are outside of acceptable ranges for functional performance. Children whose thresholds are too high tend to be underresponsive (i.e., it takes a lot of stimuli to reach the threshold, as when children don't respond to cues around them). Children whose thresholds are too low tend to be overly responsive (i.e., very little stimuli causes a reaction, as when children are distracted by every stimulus).

Principles and Features of the Behavioral Response/Self-Regulation Continuum

Children have interests, skills, and preferences about how to spend their time. These choices are not merely a matter of nervous system operations or all children would behave exactly alike. These individual behavioral differences are the subject of the behavioral sciences just as nervous system fluctuations are the subject of the neurosciences.

Goal-directed behavior has many features, including internal and external conditions for acting on a situation and a motivation to act. Infants and toddlers must have experiences that present opportunities for certain behaviors. This is a "necessary-but-not-sufficient" criterion for goal-directed behavior. Children also must have an incentive to act in a certain way. They must see that acting in certain ways will move them toward the goal, and they must have some level of interest in the act of "doing."

Children let us know their behavioral interests and tendencies by their persistence (or lack thereof) at a task. As with the neurological continuum, there is a range of performance in the center that supports adaptive behavior. There are behavioral patterns at the ends of the continuum that are maladaptive and result in unsuccessful performance. At one end of the behavioral continuum, children are so driven to perform certain rituals that these rituals interfere with the routines of daily life. At the other end of the continuum, children are so disengaged from the ongoing circumstances around them that they miss the experience of daily life routines.

The Behavioral Response/Self-Regulation Continuum shown in Figure 2.1 places Passive responses to threshold at one end of the continuum and Active responses to threshold at the other end. Passive responses to threshold mean that the child behaves consistently with neurological thresholds. For example, children with high thresholds who act in accordance with these thresholds appear unaware of their surroundings, so their high thresholds are rarely challenged. Active responses to thresholds mean that the child behaves more actively to work against thresholds. For example, children with high thresholds who counteract these thresholds continuously generate activity to create more stimuli so that their thresholds can be met more frequently. Chapter 5 provides more detailed examples.

Using this continuum within a sensory processing perspective, you can see that children have preferences for certain sensory stimuli and that sensory input can be supportive or disruptive to different children. For some children, music in the background provides sensory support, increasing the level of arousal so that play can continue uninterrupted. For other children, background music creates a distraction, interrupting play performance. Some children like the opportunity to get messy at mealtime, while others find ways to avoid putting their hands into food because it feels "yucky." Each of these behaviors provides information and insight into the child's sensory processing needs and preferences, enabling professionals to design more effective learning strategies for all children.

Constellations of Performance

The neurological threshold and behavioral response/self-regulation continua can help you understand children's performance. However, neither continuum provides sufficient information to understand the complexity of children's responses. The proposed model of sensory processing offers a wider set of possible interpretations of children's behavior by enabling you to consider the neurological and behavioral features of performance as they affect each other.

Studies using all forms of the *Sensory Profile* support this model of sensory processing (Dunn, 1997a; Ermer & Dunn, 1998; Dunn & Brown, 1997; Kientz & Dunn, 1997; Brown, Tollefson, Dunn, Cromwell, & Filion, 2001; Brown, Cromwell, Filion, Dunn, & Tollefson, in press; Dunn, Myles, & Orr, 2002; Dunn & Daniels, under revision) and enable you to consider what the performance constellations would look like at each corner of the model. The corners represent the extreme forms of responsiveness for each combination. For example, the performance constellation of Low Registration according to the conceptual model represents high neurological thresholds and a tendency to be passive in relation to these thresholds. Sensory Sensitivity represents low neurological thresholds and a tendency to be passive in relation to these thresholds. Sensation Seeking represents high neurological thresholds with a tendency to be active in relation to these thresholds, and Sensation Avoiding represents low neurological thresholds with a tendency to be active in relation to these thresholds. See Chapter 5 for details about how to use this model to interpret *Infant/Toddler Sensory Profile* data.

Rationale for Evaluating Sensory Responsiveness in Daily Life

The literature on neuroscience and sensory integrative theory provides a rich source of information as you assess, plan, and provide intervention for people with special needs (Ayres, 1975, 1980; Fisher, Murray, & Bundy, 1994). Recent neuroscience literature emphasizes modulation of input as a critical function of the central nervous system (CNS) (Kandel, Schwartz, & Jessell, 2000). The sensory integrative theory's primary postulate is that learning occurs when a person has the ability to receive accurate sensory information, process it, and use it to organize behaviors (Fisher & Murray, 1991). The literature on sensory integration places a strong emphasis on processing sensory information as a key factor in the ability to exhibit adaptive responses (Ayres, 1980; Fisher, Murray, & Bundy, 1994). The actual process of integrating sensory information is a construct discussed in both the neuroscience and sensory integration literature. However, caregivers and professionals are primarily concerned with the child's ability to manage daily life. Information that only enables the team to develop hypotheses about theoretical constructs without linking those ideas to the routines of daily life has little utility in serving the child and family. Professionals must have an understanding of the principles of neuroscience and sensory integration, and the corresponding use of that knowledge in natural contexts such as home and school.

Neuroscience

From a neuroscience perspective, modulation of input is critical to the function of the CNS. Modulation is the ability of the CNS to monitor and regulate information for the generation of appropriate responses (Dunn, 1997b). Modulation occurs by regulating habituation and sensitization responses. Habituation occurs when the CNS recognizes stimuli as familiar and non-harmful and decreases transmission among the cells. Sensitization occurs when the CNS perceives sensations as unfamiliar or potentially harmful and generates a heightened response. Both of these actions are considered part of learning in the CNS.

Another aspect of modulation is the development of thresholds for responding (Dunn, 1997b). CNS thresholds are established by genetic endowment and personal life experiences (Clarke & Clarke, 1976; Kandel, 1993). Children with poor sensory processing seem to display exceedingly high thresholds (i.e., habituation, hyposensitivity) or exceedingly low thresholds (i.e., sensitization, hypersensitivity). When thresholds are too high, children react less readily to stimuli, take a longer time to respond, and appear lethargic (Dunn, 1997a). When thresholds are too low, children react too quickly and frequently to stimuli, and appear to be overly excitable or hyperactive (Dunn, 1997a).

Sensory Integration

From a sensory integration perspective, learning occurs when a person receives accurate sensory information, processes it, and uses it to organize behaviors. When children receive inaccurate or unreliable sensory input, then their ability to process the information and create responses is disrupted (Dunn, 1991). Poor sensory processing can take many forms (Ayres, 1980) and must be inferred from observations of children's behavior and performance. Poor sensory processing can take the form of over-responsivity (e.g., becoming agitated when someone brushes against you [tactile defensiveness]) or lack of responsivity (e.g., must be tapped on the shoulder several times to gain attention). Families and service providers have hypothesized that poor sensory responsivity can affect performance (Ayres & Mailloux, 1981; Magrun, McCue, Ottenbacher, & Keefe, 1981; Ottenbacher, Scoggins, & Wayland, 1981).

Performance in Daily Life

Professionals working in early intervention and public school programs have come to realize that it is both possible and useful to apply neuroscience and sensory processing principles to children's natural life settings. In a pilot study investigating the application of sensory processing principles, Case-Smith & Bryan (1999) found that children receiving intervention using a sensory processing approach gained in mastery play and reduced non-engaged behaviors. DeGangi, Sickel, Weiner, & Kaplan (1996) studied infants with regulatory disorders and found that infants who received intervention had reductions in behavior problems, improved self-regulation, and more motor maturity three years later.

These findings provide initial evidence that there is a link between sensory processing and functional performance at school. Further work is needed to create a more direct link between functional performance and sensory processing abilities. To accomplish this goal, it is critical to have a framework for applying this theoretical knowledge in natural contexts.

The Ecology of Human Performance (EHP) framework provides this theoretical link. The EHP framework emphasizes a person's contexts as a critical variable in his or her ability to perform functional tasks in his or her life (Dunn, Brown, & McGuigan, 1994). This framework suggests that professionals must broaden the focus of data gathering to include not only information about the person's skills, but also to identify clearly what the person wants or needs to do (i.e., functional performance needs) and where the person needs to perform the task (i.e., the context). For example, washing one's face and hands before a meal presents one set of performance challenges when the person does this at home in the bathroom sink and another when he or she does it at the sink in the back of a classroom where many other students are gathering.

Three types of data need to be gathered to expand our knowledge of the application of neuroscience and sensory integration within natural contexts. First, we need data that informs us about the frame of reference being applied (i.e., sensory processing). Second, we need data about the child's functional performance. Third, we need systematic data about the context of performance so that its impact on the child's performance can be evaluated. The *Infant/Toddler Sensory Profile* directly addresses the first two of these data-gathering needs and incorporates the third by providing information from caregivers about their children's responses to sensory events in daily life.

CHAPTER 3

Research and Development of the Instrument

Brief History of the Development of the *Infant/Toddler Sensory Profile*

The *Infant/Toddler Sensory Profile* has grown out of work with children, adolescents, and adults as a means to extend the age range of the original instrument, the *Sensory Profile* (Dunn, 1999). The *Infant/Toddler Sensory Profile* follows the same tradition of asking caregivers to respond to questions about their children's frequency of responses to sensory events in daily life.

The *Sensory Profile* (designed for children 3 to 10 years of age) was originally compiled as part of research to test the application of sensory integration theory within consultative services in classrooms (Dunn, 1994; Kemmis & Dunn, 1996). In these studies, researchers used the instrument to determine which sensory processing difficulties the children seemed to be having so that consultative intervention could address the children's sensory processing needs within the classroom. These studies indicated that one could address sensory processing in the context of the daily routines and expectations of the classroom and achieve successful outcomes. Although these findings were interesting and informative for practice, therapists expressed strong interest in discovering more about the *Sensory Profile* as a measure for such purposes as contributing to comprehensive assessment or designing effective interventions. The American Occupational Therapy Foundation, the University of Kansas School of Allied Health, the Kansas Occupational Therapy Association, The Psychological Corporation, and the Federal Maternal and Child Health Bureau supported graduate students who worked on various aspects of the *Sensory Profile, Infant/Toddler Sensory Profile,* and *Adolescent/Adult Sensory Profile* development from 1993 to 2002.

After the *Sensory Profile* became available, professionals indicated that they also needed a measure for younger children. In response to this need, the process of constructing a companion measure for infants and toddlers was begun. Research took place on the *Infant/Toddler Sensory Profile* between 1998 and 2002.

Item Development

Items were developed through a series of data collection processes with families and several expert panels. Initially, researchers asked 100 parents of infants and toddlers to complete the original *Sensory Profile*, marking all that they could, and crossing out any items they felt were inappropriate for their child's age. With this initial list, researchers then constructed additional items relevant to infants and toddlers, ensuring that all sensory systems and all quadrants from Dunn's Model of Sensory Processing (see Chapter 2 for explanation of the model) would be represented. Expert panels reviewed the items and sorted them according to the quadrants, and researchers continued to revise items until panel members consistently sorted items into the same quadrants.

Then researchers conducted a pilot study with the revised form (81 items). 401 responses were obtained, and these data were used to construct the Clinical Edition of the *Infant/Toddler Sensory Profile* (58 items), that could be used by professionals in practice while the instrument was being standardized. The data from this study revealed that responsivity to sensory experiences is as relevant for younger children as it is for children 3 to 10 years of age. A complete report of this study is available in Dunn & Daniels (Dunn, W. & Daniels, D., under revision).

The *Infant/Toddler Sensory Profile—Standardization Edition* contained the same 81 items used in the pilot research study described above. Parents of children between the ages of birth and 6 months completed 36 items and parents of children between 7 and 36 months completed 81 items on the *Infant/Toddler Sensory Profile—Standardization Edition*. The final version of the *Infant/Toddler Sensory Profile* was derived from this study; the research process is summarized in this chapter.

Description of Item Categories

The results of the standardization study indicated that items could continue to be grouped in a similar way to the structure used in the *Sensory Profile*. The *Infant/Toddler Sensory Profile* contains the following groupings that reflect particular types of sensory processing sections as part of daily life.

Sensory Processing Sections

General Processing. The General Processing items reflect the child's responses related to routines and schedules (e.g., "My child's behavior deteriorates when the schedule changes.").

Auditory Processing. The items included in the Auditory Processing section measure the child's responses to things heard (e.g., "I have to speak loudly to get my child's attention.").

Visual Processing. The Visual Processing section includes items that measure the child's responses to things seen (e.g., "My child enjoys looking at shiny objects.").

Tactile Processing. The Tactile Processing section measures the child's responses to stimuli that touch the skin (e.g., "My child resists being cuddled.").

Vestibular Processing. The Vestibular Processing section measures the child's responses to movement (e.g., "My child resists having head tipped back during bathing.").

Oral Sensory Processing (7 to 36 months only). The Oral Sensory Processing section measures the child's responses to touch, taste, and smell stimuli to the mouth (e.g., "My child licks/chews on nonfood objects.").

The *Infant/Toddler Sensory Profile* also reflects the quadrants in Dunn's Model of Sensory Processing.

Quadrants

Low Registration. The items included in the Low Registration score measure the child's awareness of all types of sensation available (e.g., "My child seems unaware of wet or dirty diapers.").

Sensation Seeking. The items included in the Sensation Seeking score measure the child's interest in and pleasure with all types of sensation (e.g., "My child enjoys looking at own reflection in the mirror.").

Sensory Sensitivity. The items included in the Sensory Sensitivity score measure the child's ability to notice all types of sensation (e.g., "My child is distracted and/or has difficulty eating in noisy environments.").

Sensation Avoiding. The items included in the Sensation Avoiding score measure the child's need for controlling the amount and type of sensations available at any time (e.g., "My child avoids getting face/nose wiped.").

Low Threshold. (a combined quadrant of Sensory Sensitivity and Sensation Avoiding quadrants) This combined quadrant is relevant to some aspects of poor sensory processing, particularly for children who are fussy or who require a great deal of structure. See page 47 for further interpretive information.

Research Overview

The research on the *Infant/Toddler Sensory Profile* took place from 1998 to 2002, and included more than 1,500 children with and without disabilities between the ages of birth and 36 months and their parents.

The *Infant/Toddler Sensory Profile* standardization process took place from 2000 to 2001 and included the evaluation of more than 1,100 infants and toddlers with and without disabilities between birth and 36 months of age. The Psychological Corporation, Therapy Skill Builders, and the University of Kansas Department of Occupational Therapy Education supported graduate students who worked on various aspects of the *Infant/Toddler Sensory Profile—Standardization Edition* research project.

Examiner Selection

Over 200 professionals (occupational therapists, speech-language pathologists, school psychologists, licensed counselors, occupational therapy students, teachers, physical therapists, audiologists) participated in standardization data collection by soliciting families to complete the *Infant/Toddler Sensory Profile—Standardization Edition*. Professionals were solicited for participation from a data base of colleagues who had participated in prior studies, indicated at a workshop that they were interested in collecting data, and/or communicated their interest in participating directly to the researchers.

Description of the Sample of Children Without Disabilities That Researchers Used to Determine the Factor Structure

Examiners provided a sample of 809 children without disabilities between birth and 36 months of age. The sample contained 422 boys and 385 girls (gender not reported on 2 children). The sample included 2% Asian, 6% African American, 2% Latino, 80% Caucasian, and 2% other ethnicities (8% of the parents checked more than one ethnicity). Children were excluded from this sample if caregivers reported that the children had a medical and/or educational diagnosis, were receiving special education services, and/or were on regular prescription medication. The researchers completed the principal components factor analyses on this group of children. See pages 19–27 for further description of the Development of Scores.

Description of the Sample of Children Without Disabilities That Researchers Used to Determine Cut Scores

To better represent the general U.S population, children with ethnic backgrounds other than Caucasian were selected for the cut score group, and Caucasian children were randomly selected to complete data sets for each age group. Researchers then selected 100 children from each 6-month age group (birth to 6 month, 7 to 12 month, etc.) to comprise the cut score sample. There were only 89 children available in the 31 to 36 month age group, so this sample contained 589 children total. Tables 3.1–3.6 contain age, gender, region, race/ethnicity, income, and community information respectively for this sample.

Table 3.1

Sample by Age Groups

Age	*n*	% of Sample
0–6 months	100	17
7–12 months	100	17
13–18 months	100	17
19–24 months	100	17
25–30 months	100	17
31–36 months	89	15
Total	589	100

Table 3.2 reports the distribution of the sample by gender.

Table 3.2

Sample by Gender

Gender	*n*	% of Sample
Male	301	51.1
Female	287	48.7
Total	588	99.8
Did not report	1	0.2
Total	589	100.0

Table 3.3 reports the distribution of the sample by region.

Table 3.3
Sample by Region

Region	*n*	% of Sample
Northeast	141	24
North Central	194	33
South	103	18
West	126	21
Total	564	96
Did not report	25	4
Total	589	100

Figure 3.1 shows the breakdown of the sample by geographic regions of the United States: Northeast, North Central, South, and West.

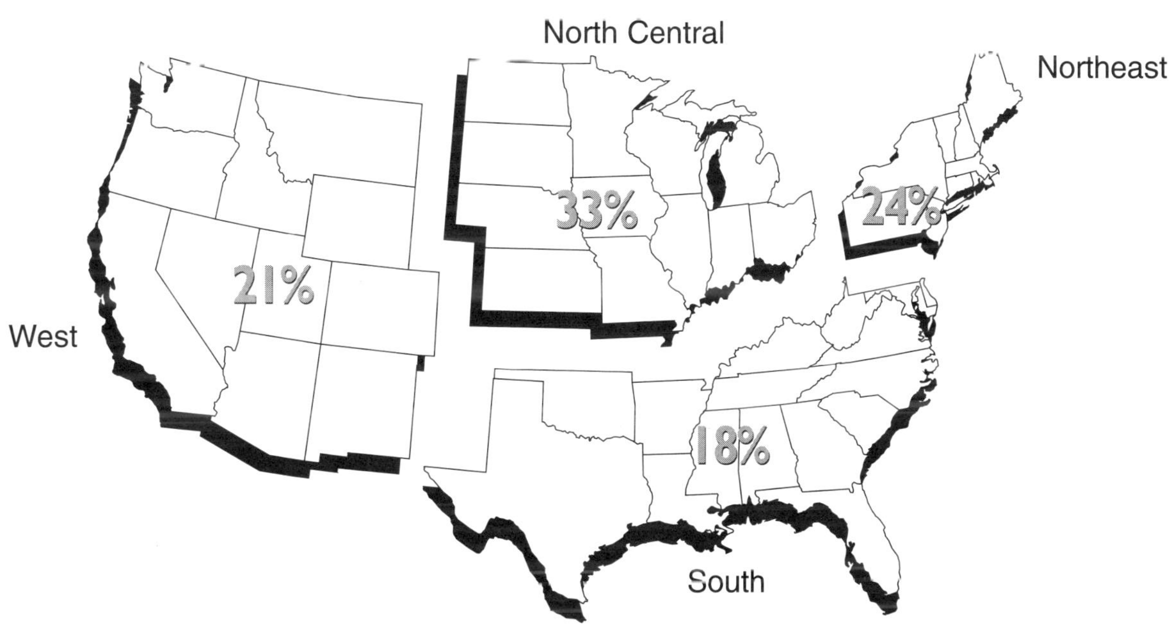

Figure 3.1 ■ **Geographic Regions of the United States for the Sample**

Note: 4% did not report region

Table 3.4 reports the distribution of the sample by race/ethnicity.

Table 3.4
Sample by Race/Ethnicity

Race/Ethnicity	*n*	% of Sample
Asian	13	2.2
African American	45	7.6
Latino	18	3.1
Caucasian	434	73.7
More than one	60	10.2
Other	18	3.1
Total	588	99.9
Did not report	1	0.2
Total	589	100.0*

*Percentages may not add to 100 due to rounding.

Table 3.5 reports the distribution of the sample by yearly income.

Table 3.5
Sample by Yearly Income

Yearly Income	*n*	% of Sample
Less than $30,000	66	11.2
$31,000 – $75,000	282	47.9
More than $76,000	227	38.5
Total	575	97.6
Did not report	14	2.4
Total	589	100.0

Table 3.6 reports the distribution of the sample by community.

Table 3.6
Sample by Community

Community	*n*	% of Sample
Rural	117	19.9
Suburban	340	57.7
Urban	93	15.8
More than one	2	0.3
Total	552	93.7
Did not report	37	6.3
Total	589	100.0

Description of the Sample of Children With Disabilities

Therapists provided data on 221 children with various disabilities and 64 children who were receiving services but who did not have a diagnosis (overall total n = 285). Table 3.7 provides a summary of the sample of children with disabilities by age and gender. More details about each disability group are provided in the chapter which discusses the comparison of disability to the sample of children without disabilities, N = 589 (see Chapter 5).

Table 3.7

Sample of Children With Disabilities by Age and Gender

Disability Group	Age Range	Boys	Girls	Totals
Services/medication	2–36 months	38	40	78
Developmental delay	7–36 months	43	25	69 (1 missing data)
Health impairments and metabolic disorders	8–35 months	16	13	29
Pervasive developmental disorder, including autism	21–36 months	20	4	24
Developmental delays and other diagnoses	11–33 months	12	6	18
Down syndrome	9–35 months	11	7	18
Sensory integrative disfunction	16–32 months	9	3	12
Language delays	19–36 months	6	2	8
Cerebral palsy	11–36 months	6	2	8
Reflux	1– 6 months	12	9	21
Totals data)		173	111	285 (1 missing

Development of Scores

Researchers scored and analyzed all *Caregiver Questionnaires* from the standardization sample of children without disabilities (N = 809) (e.g., descriptive statistics, multivariate analysis of variance, principal component factor analysis) to formulate a scoring structure and provide validity and reliability evidence.

Factor Analysis

Researchers conducted several principal components factor analyses to determine whether items clustered meaningfully into independent groupings (see Dunn & Daniels, under revision). Researchers were particularly interested in whether the *Infant/Toddler Sensory Profile* would reflect Dunn's Model of Sensory Processing. Although exploratory analyses (see below) are promising, confirmatory factor analyses will be needed to clearly establish these relationships.

Factor Analysis on Infants Birth to 6 Months of Age Without Disabilities. Researchers conducted the first set of principal components factor analyses on the sample of 150 infants birth to 6 months of age without disabilities. The initial factor analysis yielded 6 factors with Eigenvalues greater than 1.5, that accounted for 48.19% of the variance (i.e., 40% of the variation among the scores of the children could be accounted for by these factors). Using varimax rotation, a 6 factor solution was also the most interpretable, after removing only one of the original 36 items from the analysis. The final solution accounted for 48.8% of the variance. Items that had

Table 3.8

Rotated Factor Structure for Infants Birth to 6 Months of Age Without Disabilities

		Factor 1	Factor 2	Factor 3	Factor 4	Factor 5	Factor 6
Items	**Quadrant**	**Low threshold (self)**	**Low registration**	**Seeking**	**Avoiding/ High noticing**	**Low threshold (regulation)**	**Context awareness**
% of variance		**9.29%**	**9.18%**	**9.06%**	**8.37%**	**7.79%**	**5.11%**
General Processing 1	Sensation Seeking			.667			
General Processing 2	Low Registration				-.478		
General Processing 3	Low Registration		.610				
General Processing 4	Sensory Sensitivity					.431	
General Processing 5	Sensory Sensitivity					.523	
General Processing 6	Sensory Sensitivity					.481	
Auditory Processing 7	Low Registration		.545				
Auditory Processing 8	Low Registration				-.461		
Auditory Processing 9	Low Registration		.610				
Auditory Processing 10	Low Registration		.493				
Auditory Processing 11	Sensation Seeking			.736			
Auditory Processing 12	Low Registration		.622				
Auditory Processing 13	Sensory Sensitivity	.408			.440		
Auditory Processing 14	Sensory Sensitivity					.470	-.439
Auditory Processing 15	Low Registration		.646				
Visual Processing 16	Sensation Seeking			.729			
Visual Processing 17	Sensation Seeking			.778			
Visual Processing 18	Low Registration		.481				
Visual Processing 19	Sensory Sensitivity						.520
Visual Processing 20	Low Registration				.592		
Visual Processing 21	Sensory Sensitivity			-.422			
Visual Processing 22	Sensation Avoiding						-.516

Table 3.8 *(continued)*

Rotated Factor Structure for Infants Birth to 6 Months of Age Without Disabilities

		Factor 1	Factor 2	Factor 3	Factor 4	Factor 5	Factor 6
Items	**Quadrant**	**Low threshold (self)**	**Low registration**	**Seeking**	**Avoiding/ High noticing**	**Low threshold (regulation)**	**Context awareness**
% of variance		**9.29%**	**9.18%**	**9.06%**	**8.37%**	**7.79%**	**5.11%**
Tactile Processing 23*	Low Registration						
Tactile Processing 24	Sensation Avoiding				.710		
Tactile Processing 25	Sensory Sensitivity	.726					
Tactile Processing 26	Sensation Avoiding	.716					
Tactile Processing 27	Sensory Sensitivity	.581					
Tactile Processing 28	Sensation Avoiding				.736		
Vestibular Processing 29	Low Registration						.402
Vestibular Processing 30	Sensation Seeking			.602			
Vestibular Processing 31	Low Registration					-.509	
Vestibular Processing 32	Sensation Seeking					-.594	
Vestibular Processing 33	Sensory Sensitivity	.568					
Vestibular Processing 34	Sensory Sensitivity					.695	
Vestibular Processing 35	Sensation Avoiding	.709					
Vestibular Processing 36	Sensory Sensitivity	.458					

*Item weights are less than .40 in the factor structure.

weaker relationships within the factor structure (i.e., with commonalities of <.40) were eliminated from the analysis (Gorsuch, 1983). Table 3.8 displays the rotated matrix for the final solution, listing only weights greater than .40.

Factor Analysis on Older Infants and Toddlers Without Disabilities. Researchers conducted the second set of principal components factor analyses on the sample of 659 children 7 to 36 months of age without disabilities. The initial factor analysis yielded 10 factors with Eigenvalues greater than 1.5, that accounted for 40.5% of the variance. Using varimax rotation, it was determined that a 6 factor solution was the most interpretable; this solution accounted for 44.3% of the variance. The researchers eliminated 38 items before attaining the final solution. Table 3.9 displays the rotated matrix for the final solution, listing only weights greater than .40.

Factor Analysis on Children With Various Disabilities. Researchers conducted a principal components factor analysis using the data from diagnosed disability groups to identify patterns that emerge with children who have disabilities. A difference between these patterns and those that emerge from the children without disabilities might provide possible important considerations for using the *Infant/Toddler Sensory Profile* in the assessment process. There were 285 children 7 to 36 months of age with various disabilities (see Chapter 5 for specific demographics). 48.5% of the variance was accounted for in the varimax rotation with 7 factors (Eigenvalues above 1.5). Table 3.10 displays the rotated matrix for the final solution, listing only weights greater than .40.

Impressions From Factor Analyses

All of the factor analyses seem to reflect constructs in Dunn's Model of Sensory Processing. The items on the *Infant/Toddler Sensory Profile* do not load according to their sensory systems, but rather according to their sensory processing characteristic. Specifically, each of the analyses includes factors in which items cluster based on thresholds and behavioral responses (i.e., Low Registration and Sensation Seeking, which are the high threshold components of Dunn's Model of Sensory Processing, and Sensory Sensitivity and Sensation Avoiding, which reflect low threshold components of Dunn's Model of Sensory Processing).

So, in a general way, the same constructs emerge from the infant/toddler data as have emerged from the original *Sensory Profile* for children ages 3 to 10 years (Dunn, 1999) and the *Adolescent/Adult Sensory Profile* (Brown et. al., 2001; Pohl, Dunn, & Brown, submitted; Brown & Dunn, 2002). However, there are unique characteristics in the organization of the factor structures for these children that seem to reflect their evolving abilities to manage the myriad of sensory inputs throughout the day.

Specifically, the data for children ages 7 to 36 months old (n = 659) is closest in organization to the children and adult data, with Sensation Seeking as the largest factor (i.e., largest % of variance), and other quadrant factors being less prominent. The infants display a more evenly distributed pattern across the factors (i.e., equal contributions to the variance), with both Low Registration and Low Threshold factors being somewhat larger than the Sensation Seeking factor. Perhaps the unique pattern in the youngest infants (birth to 6 months) reflects their early experiences of discovering sensations outside the mother's womb. Because many sensations are unfamiliar, it is possible that the infants have either a high rate of responding (reflected in Low Threshold responses), or they fail to recognize stimuli that might be important, therefore appearing to have Low Registration. The fact that this pattern of equal contribution to variance shifts toward the pattern we see in children and adults as we examine children ages 7 to 36 months suggests that these early patterns are reflecting early developmental experiences. Longitudinal studies need to be conducted to verify this hypothesis.

It is informative to see that in the factor structure for children with disabilities the items cluster together based on thresholds just as the items clustered for the children without disabilities. However, Low Registration and Low Threshold factors are more prominent than Sensation Seeking (based on the % of variance contribution). Perhaps this shift in the weighting of these factors reflects differences in how children with disabilities manage sensory events in daily life. With Low Registration (i.e., lack of noticing) and Low Threshold (i.e., hypervigilance in noticing) more heavily weighted than Sensation Seeking, perhaps we see the children's struggle to manage and prioritize incoming stimuli. While children without disabilities seem to use seeking strategies to gather information and learn, perhaps children with disabilities must either struggle to notice the right stimuli or face the possibility of being overwhelmed by stimuli.

Development of the Classification System and Cut Scores

Two classification systems were derived, one for children ages birth to 6 months and one for children ages 7 to 36 months. The classification system provides an estimate of the child's likely performance in each sensory processing section or quadrant when compared to peers. Researchers derived the cut scores from the sample of children without disabilities ($N = 589$) between the ages of birth and 36 months.

Note: Cut scores for children birth to 6 months were established using 100 babies without disabilities, and cut scores for children 7 to 36 months were established using 489 children without disabilities.

We examined the frequency distribution of children's scores and verified that the scores were normally distributed (i.e., would reflect a bell curve distribution). It is common practice to select cut scores that correspond to various standard deviations below and above the mean in a normal distribution. Such a cut score represents the 16th percentile. The distribution of scores on the *Infant/Toddler Sensory Profile—Clinical Edition* were not normally distributed and therefore the cut scores on that version were based on percentiles. Since the data for the final edition of the *Infant/Toddler Sensory Profile* proved to be close to a normal distribution, researchers decided it was appropriate to use standard deviations to represent cut scores.

The classification system for children ages **birth to 6 months** describes children's sensory processing abilities for each quadrant and combined quadrant as either:

- Typical Performance or
- Consult and Follow-up.

The classification system for children ages **7 to 36 months** describes children's sensory processing abilities for each quadrant, combined quadrant and sensory processing section as:

- Typical Performance,
- Probable Difference, or
- Definite Difference.

A **new feature** of the scores for the *Infant/Toddler Sensory Profile* is that a child can receive a score at either end of a continuum, with the Typical Response score falling within the scoring range. Scores at the higher end of the scoring continuum indicate the child is LESS responsive than peers (i.e., higher points for Almost Never), while scores at the lower end of the scoring continuum indicate the child is MORE responsive than peers (i.e., lower points for Almost Always).

Table 3.9

Rotated Factor Structure for Children 7 to 36 Months of Age Without Disabilities

		Factor 1	Factor 2	Factor 3	Factor 4	Factor 5	Factor 6
Items	**Quadrant**	**Seeking**	**Low threshold (context)**	**Low threshold (self)**	**Oral sensory**	**Low registration**	**Avoiding**
% of variance		**11.54%**	**8.02%**	**7.31%**	**6.50%**	**6.49%**	**4.47%**
General Processing 1*	Sensory Sensitivity						
General Processing 2	Sensation Avoiding						.800
General Processing 3	Sensation Avoiding						.806
Auditory Processing 4	Low Registration					.690	
Auditory Processing 5	Low Registration					.685	
Auditory Processing 6	Sensation Seeking	.550					
Auditory Processing 7	Low Registration					.658	
Auditory Processing 8*	Sensory Sensitivity						
Auditory Processing 9*	Sensory Sensitivity						
Auditory Processing 10*	Low Registration						
Auditory Processing 11	Sensation Avoiding						.522
Auditory Processing 12	Sensation Seeking	.614					
Auditory Processing 13	Low Registration					.629	
Visual Processing 14	Sensation Seeking	.618					
Visual Processing 15	Sensation Seeking	.620					
Visual Processing 16	Low Registration					.517	
Visual Processing 17*	Sensation Avoiding						
Visual Processing 18*	Low Registration						
Visual Processing 19	Sensation Seeking	.554					
Visual Processing 20	Sensation Seeking	.456					
Tactile Processing 21	Sensation Avoiding			.509			
Tactile Processing 22	Sensory Sensitivity			.488			
Tactile Processing 23	Sensation Avoiding			.640			
Tactile Processing 24	Sensory Sensitivity			.640			

Table 3.9 *(continued)*

Rotated Factor Structure for Children 7 to 36 Months of Age Without Disabilities

		Factor 1	Factor 2	Factor 3	Factor 4	Factor 5	Factor 6
Items	**Quadrant**	**Seeking**	**Low threshold (context)**	**Low threshold (self)**	**Oral sensory**	**Low registration**	**Avoiding**
% of variance		**11.54%**	**8.02%**	**7.31%**	**6.50%**	**6.49%**	**4.47%**
Tactile Processing 25	Sensation Avoiding			.561			
Tactile Processing 26	Sensory Sensitivity		.576				
Tactile Processing 27	Sensation Avoiding		.564				
Tactile Processing 28*	Sensory Sensitivity						
Tactile Processing 29	Sensory Sensitivity		.711				
Tactile Processing 30	Sensation Seeking		.534				
Tactile Processing 31	Sensation Seeking	.521					
Tactile Processing 32	Sensation Seeking	.515					
Tactile Processing 33*	Low Registration						
Tactile Processing 34	Sensation Seeking	.623					
Tactile Processing 35	Sensation Seeking	.638					
Vestibular Processing 36*	Low Registration						
Vestibular Processing 37	Sensation Seeking	.631					
Vestibular Processing 38	Sensation Seeking	.603					
Vestibular Processing 39	Sensory Sensitivity			.483			
Vestibular Processing 40	Sensation Avoiding			.565			
Vestibular Processing 41	Sensory Sensitivity			.476			
Oral Sensory Processing 42	Sensation Seeking				.768		
Oral Sensory Processing 43	Sensation Seeking				.780		
Oral Sensory Processing 44	Low Registration				.462		
Oral Sensory Processing 45*	Sensation Avoiding						
Oral Sensory Processing 46	Sensation Avoiding			.577			
Oral Sensory Processing 47*	Low Registration						
Oral Sensory Processing 48*	Sensation Avoiding						

*Item weights are less than .40 in the factor structure.

Table 3.10

Rotated Factor Structure for Children With Various Disabilities

		Factor 1	Factor 2	Factor 3	Factor 4	Factor 5	Factor 6	Factor 7
Items	**Quadrant**	**Low registration**	**Low threshold**	**Seeking**	**Low threshold (self)**	**Seeking/ taste smell**	**Seeking/ objects**	**Oral sensory**
% of variance		**11.59%**	**8.50%**	**6.86%**	**6.07%**	**5.44%**	**5.18%**	**4.89%**
General Processing 1	Sensory Sensitivity		.500					
General Processing 2	Sensation Avoiding	.558						
General Processing 3	Sensation Avoiding	.472	.418					
Auditory Processing 4	Low Registration	.719						
Auditory Processing 5	Low Registration	.789						
Auditory Processing 6	Sensation Seeking			.423				
Auditory Processing 7	Low Registration	.781						
Auditory Processing 8	Sensory Sensitivity		.584					
Auditory Processing 9	Sensory Sensitivity		.445					
Auditory Processing 10	Low Registration	.742						
Auditory Processing 11*	Sensation Avoiding							
Auditory Processing 12*	Sensation Seeking							
Auditory Processing 13	Low Registration	.817		.523				
Visual Processing 14	Sensation Seeking						.638	
Visual Processing 15	Sensation Seeking						.674	
Visual Processing 16	Low Registration	.691						
Visual Processing 17	Sensation Avoiding	.582						
Visual Processing 18	Low Registration	.541						
Visual Processing 19	Sensation Seeking	-.486						
Visual Processing 20*	Sensation Seeking							
Tactile Processing 21	Sensation Avoiding		.560					
Tactile Processing 22	Sensory Sensitivity				.484			
Tactile Processing 23	Sensation Avoiding				.477			
Tactile Processing 24	Sensory Sensitivity				.614			

Table 3.10 *(continued)*

Rotated Factor Structure for Children With Various Disabilities

Items	Quadrant	Factor 1 Low registration	Factor 2 Low threshold	Factor 3 Seeking	Factor 4 Low threshold (self)	Factor 5 Seeking/ taste smell	Factor 6 Seeking/ objects	Factor 7 Oral sensory
% of variance		**11.59%**	**8.50%**	**6.86%**	**6.07%**	**5.44%**	**5.18%**	**4.89%**
Tactile Processing 25	Sensation Avoiding		.629					
Tactile Processing 26	Sensory Sensitivity		.628					
Tactile Processing 27	Sensation Avoiding		.630					
Tactile Processing 28	Sensory Sensitivity		.535					
Tactile Processing 29	Sensory Sensitivity		.558					
Tactile Processing 30*	Sensation Seeking							
Tactile Processing 31	Sensation Seeking			.569				
Tactile Processing 32	Sensation Seeking					.467		
Tactile Processing 33	Low Registration	.415						
Tactile Processing 34	Sensation Seeking			.558				
Tactile Processing 35	Sensation Seeking			.630				
Vestibular Processing 36	Low Registration						.523	
Vestibular Processing 37	Sensation Seeking			.540				
Vestibular Processing 38	Sensation Seeking			.483				
Vestibular Processing 39	Sensory Sensitivity				.600			
Vestibular Processing 40	Sensation Avoiding				.589			
Vestibular Processing 41	Sensory Sensitivity		.466					
Oral Sensory Processing 42	Sensation Seeking						.634	
Oral Sensory Processing 43	Sensation Seeking						.665	
Oral Sensory Processing 44	Low Registration	.400						
Oral Sensory Processing 45	Sensation Avoiding							.737
Oral Sensory Processing 46	Sensation Avoiding				.565			
Oral Sensory Processing 47	Low Registration				.413			
Oral Sensory Processing 48	Sensation Avoiding							.743

*Item weights are less than .40 in the factor structure.

Types of Scores and Classification System

Sensory Processing Section and Quadrant Raw Scores

Table 3.11 reports the mean raw scores and standard deviations by sensory processing section for each age group. Table 3.12 reports the mean raw scores and standard deviations by quadrant for each age group. All information is derived from the *Infant/Toddler Sensory Profile* selected standardization sample of children without disabilities ($N = 589$). Data for children birth to 6 months are reported in 3-month increments; for children 7 to 36 months in 6-month increments.

For most of the sensory processing section and quadrant groupings, there was very little difference in the mean raw scores across the age groups. These scores indicate that children's sensory processing abilities remain at the same level across this age range. Chapter 5 contains information on interpreting scores for children.

Table 3.11

Mean Raw Scores and Standard Deviations for the *Infant/Toddler Sensory Profile* Sensory Processing Sections by Age

	General		Auditory		Visual		Tactile		Vestibular		Oral	
Months old	Mean	*SD*	Mean	*SD*	Mean	*SD*	Mean	*SD*	Mean	*SD*	Mean	*SD*
0–3	N/A*	N/A*	N/A*	N/A*	N/A*	N/A*	N/A*	N/A*	N/A*	N/A*	N/A**	N/A**
4–6	N/A*	N/A*	N/A*	N/A*	N/A*	N/A*	N/A*	N/A*	N/A*	N/A*	N/A**	N/A**
7–12	N/A*	N/A*	39.08	3.51	22.47	3.29	54.82	6.15	19.61	2.78	33.12	4.81
13–18	N/A*	N/A*	38.98	3.55	22.93	3.40	54.73	6.11	20.26	2.44	34.70	4.82
19–24	N/A*	N/A*	38.62	4.48	23.68	3.88	54.66	6.81	20.08	2.90	35.49	4.68
25–30	N/A*	N/A*	38.90	4.12	24.04	3.20	56.79	6.22	20.75	2.45	36.18	4.06
31–36	N/A*	N/A*	39.43	5.35	25.30	3.93	58.40	6.85	21.59	2.85	37.15	4.83

*No cut score available because these item groupings had low reliability.

**No items for this section for children birth to 6 months.

Table 3.12

Mean Raw Scores and Standard Deviations for the *Infant/Toddler Sensory Profile* Quadrants by Age

	Sensation Seeking		Sensory Sensitivity		Low Registration		Sensation Avoiding		Low Threshold	
Months old	Mean	*SD*	Mean	*SD*	Mean	*SD*	Mean	*SD*	Mean	*SD*
0–3	12.47	4.31	51.93	5.18	43.48	4.96	22.23	2.57	74.18	6.89
4–6	9.16	3.05	49.66	6.78	46.64	4.59	21.20	3.02	71.16	9.10
7–12	33.57	8.00	46.51	5.11	49.94	3.86	50.11	5.53	96.81	9.85
13–18	33.47	8.22	47.11	4.66	50.28	3.78	50.88	5.30	97.89	9.26
19–24	36.20	8.62	46.04	5.07	49.76	3.93	50.00	5.42	96.04	9.88
25–30	37.97	7.56	46.48	5.46	50.64	3.48	50.21	5.71	96.67	10.35
31–36	41.42	10.90	46.96	6.05	50.48	4.19	51.45	5.70	98.37	10.99

Cut Scores Birth to 6 Months

Cut scores for children ages birth to 6 months were determined for each quadrant in the following manner (See Figure 5.1 on page 40 for a graphic representation of the classification system for children ages birth to 6 months.):

- **Consult and Follow-up** corresponds to scores outside + or –1 *SD* from the mean for children without disabilities. Remember: infants can be more responsive (have lower scores) or less responsive (have higher scores) than peers. Therefore, there is a cut score at both ends of the continuum, corresponding to below –1 *SD* from the mean and above +1 *SD* from the mean respectively.
- **Typical Performance** corresponds to scores at or between + or –1 *SD* from the mean for children without disabilities.

Note: For children ages birth to 6 months there are two sets of cut scores on the *Summary Score Sheet* for the Low Registration quadrant. This is due to the fact that low registration behaviors decrease in frequency for children ages birth to 6 months (i.e., increase awareness of stimuli).

Cut Scores 7 to 36 Months

Cut scores for children ages 7 to 36 months were determined for each section and quadrant in the following manner (See Figure 5.2 on page 40 for a graphic representation of the classification system for children ages 7 to 36 months.):

- **Definite Difference** corresponds to scores outside + or –2 *SD* from the mean for children without disabilities.
  - Scores above the point 2 *SD* above the mean represent **underresponsiveness** when compared to peers.
  - Scores below the point 2 *SD* below the mean represent **overresponsiveness** when compared to peers.
- **Probable Difference** corresponds to scores within the 1 to 2 *SD* range; specifically:
  - Scores at or below the point 2 *SD* above the mean, but higher than 1 *SD* above the mean, for children without disabilities represent **underresponsiveness**.
  - Scores at or above the point 2 *SD* below the mean, but lower than 1 *SD* below the mean, for children without disabilities represent **overresponsiveness**.
- **Typical Performance** corresponds to scores at or between + or –1 *SD* from the mean for children without disabilities.

Several quadrants/sections have different cut scores depending on the child's age. The *Infant/Toddler Sensory Profile* shows some developmental trends in the data for children 7 to 36 months. Specifically, there are 3 scores that shifted during the infant/toddler period: Sensation Seeking, Tactile Processing, and Oral Sensory Processing. You will see on the *Summary Score Sheet* that, for Sensation Seeking, Tactile Processing and Oral Sensory Processing, you must select the row corresponding to the child's age when recording the child's score. These developmental trends are also highlighted in Appendix A. Appendix A contains three reproducible growth charts reflecting these developmental trends (for more information about the growth charts see page 47).

This method for determining cut scores was selected for several reasons. First, these decisions are based on the data collected from a large sample of children and therefore represent actual trends in children's performance in the population sampled. Second, you can use the *Infant/Toddler Sensory Profile* to determine whether sensory processing difficulties are interfering with a particular child's performance. By using the scores from the children without disabilities (who scored more homogeneously than groups with disabilities), your ability to identify children who may need further attention is maximized. (See Appendix B for a graphic comparison of mean and standard deviation patterns across disability groups.)

Remember, the *Infant/Toddler Sensory Profile* only provides one source of information; by identifying a Probable Difference group, you can study all the assessment data, consider sensory processing correlates, and take a smaller chance of overlooking this aspect of a child's difficulty.

CHAPTER 4

Administration Instructions and Scoring

General Testing Considerations

Before using the *Infant/Toddler Sensory Profile*, familiarize yourself with the *User's Manual* and the *Caregiver Questionnaire*. Orient yourself to the instrument's purpose as well as to the items and rating scale on the *Caregiver Questionnaire* in case the caregiver has any questions. Follow all administration and scoring procedures to maintain test reliability and to ensure that interpretations of results are based on the standard procedures used to develop this instrument.

Caregiver Questionnaire *Layout*

The *Caregiver Questionnaire* was designed to be user-friendly for caregivers as well as informative to professionals. It contains instructions and a response key for caregivers, and item-specific information such as icons. The *Caregiver Questionnaire* contains two versions of the questions, one version for children ages birth to 6 months and another version for children ages 7 to 36 months (see Figure 4.1).

The first column in Figure 4.1 contains an icon that indicates the associated quadrant for each item. The key shown in Figure 4.2 indicates the quadrant the icon represents. The second column indicates the actual item number.

You may use the first column to further refine your interpretations of a child's sensory processing abilities by looking at the scores in relation to each quadrant.

Administering the Infant/Toddler Sensory Profile

There are three general ways in which you can administer the *Infant/Toddler Sensory Profile*.

1. Send the *Caregiver Questionnaire* to the caregiver with a cover letter explaining the purpose of the instrument, including the importance of matching the child's age range to the correct section of the questionnaire. Be sure to include your phone number in case the caregiver has questions about the form.
2. Have the caregiver complete the form in your office or clinic while you are evaluating the child.

Item		A. General Processing	ALMOST ALWAYS	FREQUENTLY	OCCASIONALLY	SELDOM	ALMOST NEVER
	1	My child is active throughout the day.					
—	2	My child stays quiet and calm in an active environment when compared to same age children.					
—	3	My child is unaware of people coming in and going out of the room.					
	4	My child's behavior deteriorates when the schedule changes.					
	5	My child has difficulty getting to sleep and is easily awakened.					
	6	My child is irritable when compared to same age children.					

Comments

Figure 4.1 ■ **Item Layout**

ICON KEY	
—	Low Registration
	Sensation Seeking
	Sensory Sensitivity
|	Sensation Avoiding

Figure 4.2 ■ **Icon Key**

3. Help the caregiver fill out the *Caregiver Questionnaire*. Use this procedure if the caregiver has difficulty reading because of language differences or reading disabilities.

If the caregiver asks questions, provide clarification without indicating a correct response. Encourage the caregiver to consider how frequently the child engages in the behaviors of interest.

Establishing a Rapport

It is important that caregivers understand that the information you are requesting is critical to your work and that the time they take to complete the materials is invaluable to the process of planning for their child. If you send materials to the caregiver's home, include a letter with a brief explanation of the instrument and why the information is important to the assessment process. Explain the caregiver's central role in providing a picture of the child's performance and the caregiver's concerns about daily life.

Specific Administration Procedures

Before giving the *Caregiver Questionnaire* to the caregiver, fill in the child's name and birth date on top of the first page as well as your name (Service Provider's Name) and discipline. Explain the purpose of the *Infant/Toddler Sensory Profile* to the caregiver (or provide that information in a cover letter). Have the caregiver write his or her name, relationship to the child, the date, and answer the other questions on the first page of the form. Ask the caregiver to read the items and check the box that best describes the frequency with which he or she sees the behaviors in the child. Instruct the caregiver to use the following key to mark responses.

Almost Always: When presented with the opportunity, your child **almost always** responds in this manner, 90% or more of the time.

Frequently: When presented with the opportunity, your child **frequently** responds in this manner, about 75% of the time.

Occasionally: When presented with the opportunity, your child **occasionally** responds in this manner, about 50% of the time.

Seldom: When presented with the opportunity, your child **seldom** responds in this manner, about 25% of the time.

Almost Never: When presented with the opportunity, your child **almost never** responds in this manner, 10% or less of the time.

Emphasize the importance of completing all the items. Encourage the caregiver to provide additional comments about the child's behaviors in the Comments sections. Explain to the caregiver that he or she needs only provide information about the child's behaviors and that you will fill in the section raw score totals as indicated.

Once the caregiver has completed the form, make sure all items have been answered and that the caregiver has answered all the questions at the end of the questionnaire. If the caregiver has left any item blank, ask him or her to complete the item. You may need to clarify the item for the caregiver.

Note: If any item is left blank, you cannot compute a raw score total for that section or for any quadrant that contains that item. If the caregiver marks an X next to the item number because he or she has determined that a particular item is not applicable due to age or the child has not had the opportunity to experience the behavior, you cannot compute a raw score total for that section or for any quadrant that contains that item.

Scoring the *Caregiver Questionnaire*

After you have made sure each item has a response, score each response according to the following:

Almost Always = 1 point

Frequently = 2 points

Occasionally = 3 points

Seldom = 4 points

Almost Never = 5 points

If the caregiver places a mark between two categories, record the more frequent score:

Between Almost Never and Seldom, record Seldom (4 points)

Between Seldom and Occasionally, record Occasionally (3 points)

Between Occasionally and Frequently, record Frequently (2 points)

Between Frequently and Almost Always, record Almost Always (1 point)

To determine the sensory processing section raw score total, add the item scores for each section as indicated (7 to 36 month old children only). Write that score in the box labeled Section Raw Score Total following each section (see Figure 4.3).

A new feature of the scores for the *Infant/Toddler Sensory Profile* is that a child can receive a score at either end of a continuum. Scores at the higher end of the scoring continuum indicate the child is less responsive than peers (i.e., higher points for Almost Never), while scores at the lower end of the scoring continuum indicate the child is more responsive than peers (i.e., lower points for Almost Always.).

Item		B. Auditory Processing	Almost Always	Frequently	Occasionally	Seldom	Almost Never
—	4	I have to speak loudly to get my child's attention.		X2			
—	5	I have to touch my child to gain attention.	X1				
S	6	My child enjoys making sounds with his/her mouth.			X3		
—	7	My child takes a long time to respond, even to familiar voices.			X3		
@	8	My child startles easily at sound, compared to other children the same age.				X4	
@	9	My child is distracted and/or has difficulty eating in noisy environments.					X5
—	10	My child ignores me when I am talking.		X2			
|	11	My child tries to escape from noisy environments.				X4	
S	12	My child finds ways to make noise with toys.		X2			
—	13	It takes a long time for my child to respond to his/her name when it is called.	X1				
		Section Raw Score Total			27		

Comments

Figure 4.3 ■ **Scoring the *Caregiver Questionnaire***

Using the *Summary Score Sheet*

The *Summary Score Sheet* includes space to record demographic information about the child, the Quadrant Grid and Quadrant Summary for children birth to 6 months old, and the Quadrant Grid, Quadrant Summary, and Sensory Processing Section Summary for children 7 to 36 months old. Fill in the demographic information on the first page of the *Summary Score Sheet,* including the child's name, gender, the date, who completed the *Caregiver Questionnaire* and his or her relationship to the child, and the service provider's name and discipline. Complete both checklists (child's conditions and services received) and record any referral concerns and additional comments in the space provided at the bottom of the page.

Transfer any pertinent caregiver comments from the Comments sections to the bottom of the front page of the *Summary Score Sheet.*

Computing Chronological Age

Calculate the child's chronological age by subtracting the child's birth date from the date the *Caregiver Questionnaire* was completed. In doing so, remember:

1. When borrowing days from months, always borrow 30 days regardless of the month.
2. When borrowing months from years, always borrow 12 months.

For example, the chronological age of a child whose caregiver filled out the questionnaire on June 18, 2002, and whose birth date is June 20, 2001 is 0 years 11 months and 28 days (see Figure 4.4).

	YEAR	MONTH	DAY
Date Tested	~~02~~ 01	~~05~~ 16 ~~04~~	~~18~~ 48
Date of Birth	01	05	20
Chronological Age	0	11	28

Figure 4.4 ■ **Computing Chronological Age**

Completing the Quadrant Grid

The Quadrant Grid for children ages birth to 6 months is located on page 2 and for children ages 7 to 36 months is located on page 3 of the *Summary Score Sheet*. Each quadrant is divided into two columns (see Figure 4.5). The first column contains the item number that corresponds to the item number on the *Caregiver Questionnaire*. The second column is where you write the item raw scores.

7 to 36 Months Summary Score Sheet

Quadrant Grid

Instructions: Transfer from the Caregiver Questionnaire (7 to 36 months) the Item raw score that corresponds with each item listed. Add the Raw Score column to get the Quadrant Raw Score Total for each quandrant.

QUADRANT 1 — Low Registration

Item	Raw Score
4	3
5	4
7	5
10	4
13	4
16	5
18	3
33	4
36	4
44	5
47	3
Quadrant Raw Score Total	44

QUADRANT 2 — Sensation Seeking

Item	Raw Score
6	4
12	4
14	4
15	5
19	3
20	4
31	4
32	3
34	4
35	5
37	4
38	3
42	4
43	5
Quadrant Raw Score Total	56

QUADRANT 3 — Sensory Sensitivity

Item	Raw Score
1	2
8	1
9	2
22	1
24	2
26	3
28	1
29	2
30	3
39	1
41	1
Quadrant Raw Score Total	19

QUADRANT 4 — Sensation Avoiding

Item	Raw Score
2	1
3	1
11	2
17	3
21	1
23	1
25	3
27	2
40	2
45	1
46	2
48	2
Quadrant Raw Score Total	21

ICON KEY

—	Low Registration
S	Sensation Seeking
⑥	Sensory Sensitivity
|	Sensation Avoiding

Figure 4.5 ■ **Scoring the Quadrant Grid**

To calculate the child's quadrant raw score totals, transfer item raw scores from the *Caregiver Questionnaire* to the corresponding item number on the Quadrant Grid. Add the Raw Score column for each quadrant and record the totals in the box labeled Quadrant Raw Score Total.

Computing the Low Threshold Raw Score Total

To compute the Low Threshold Raw Score Total, add the Sensory Sensitivity and Sensation Avoiding Quadrant Raw Score Totals together (see Figure 4.6) and write the total in the box labeled Low Threshold Raw Score Total.

If one of the Low Threshold scores (Sensation Avoiding or Sensory Sensitivity) ends up in the Typical Performance range, the combined Low Threshold score will not be useful. This score is only relevant when both the Sensation Avoiding and Sensory Sensitivity quadrant scores are outside the Typical Performance range, as a means for

Birth to 6 Months Summary Score Sheet

Quadrant Grid

Instructions: Transfer from the Caregiver Questionnaire (Birth to 6 months) the item raw score that corresponds with each item listed. Add the Raw Score column to get the Quadrant Raw Score Total for each quadrant.

QUADRANT 1	
Low Registration	
Item	Raw Score
2	1
3	3
7	1
8	2
9	1
10	3
12	1
15	1
18	2
20	2
23	2
29	3
31	1
Quadrant Raw Score Total	23

QUADRANT 2	
Sensation Seeking	
Item	Raw Score
1	3
11	1
16	2
17	3
30	3
32	3
Quadrant Raw Score Total	15

QUADRANT 3	
Sensory Sensitivity	
Item	Raw Score
4	4
5	5
6	4
13	4
14	3
19	3
21	4
25	3
27	3
33	3
34	4
36	1
Quadrant Raw Score Total	41

QUADRANT 4	
Sensation Avoiding	
Item	Raw Score
22	2
24	3
26	4
28	4
35	3
Quadrant Raw Score Total	16

ICON KEY
Low Registration
Sensation Seeking
Sensory Sensitivity
Sensation Avoiding

Low Threshold (combined quadrant score)

Instructions: Add Sensory Sensitivity and Sensation Avoiding Quadrant Raw Score Totals to get the Low Threshold Raw Score Total

Low Threshold Raw Score Total	41 + 16 = 57

Figure 4.6 ■ **Computing the Low Threshold Raw Score Total**

characterizing a Low Threshold condition. Merging a Typical Performance score with a score outside the Typical Performance range will mask the pertinent contrast. In these cases, use the separate quadrant scores to interpret the child's performance, taking full advantage of the specific information provided by the quadrant scores.

Completing the Quadrant Summary

The Quadrant Summary is located on page 2 of the *Summary Score Sheet* for children ages birth to 6 months and page 3 of the *Summary Score Sheet* for children ages 7 to 36 months. The Quadrant Summary provides an additional way to consider the child's scores. The quadrants reveal patterns related to the child's responsivity to stimuli in the environments based on Dunn's Model of Sensory Processing (Dunn, 1997a). Transfer the child's score for each quadrant to the corresponding Quadrant Raw Score Total column of the Quadrant Summary. Plot the child's quadrant raw score total by marking an X in the appropriate classification column, (Typical Performance or Consult and Follow-up for children ages birth to 6 months and Typical Performance, Probable Difference, or Definite Difference for children ages 7 to 36 months) corresponding to the raw score total for each quadrant.

Several quadrants have different cut scores depending on the child's age. Make sure you transfer the Quadrant Raw Score Totals to the appropriate age band for each quadrant (See Figure 4.7).

Quadrant Summary

Instructions: Transfer the Quadrant Raw Score Totals from the 7 to 36 months Quadrant Grid to the corresponding Quadrant Raw Score Total box for the appropriate ages. Plot these totals by marking an X in the appropriate classification column (Typical Performance, Probable Difference, Definite Difference)*.

		Less Than Others ←			→ More Than Others	
Quadrant	**Quadrant Raw Score Total**	**Definite Difference**	**Probable Difference**	**Typical Performance**	**Probable Difference**	**Definite Difference**
1. Low Registration (7–36 months)	54 /55	**	55	X ---------- 46	45 ---------- 43	42 ---------- 11
2. Sensation Seeking (7–12 months)	/70	70 ---------- 44	43 ---------- 36	35 ---------- 19	18 ---------- 14	**
2. Sensation Seeking (13–18 months)	33 /70	70 ---------- 46	45 ---------- 38	37--X---- 20	19 ---------- 14	**
2. Sensation Seeking (19–24 months)	/70	70 ---------- 50	49 ---------- 42	41 ---------- 25	24 ---------- 16	15 ---------- 14
2. Sensation Seeking (25–30 months)	/70	70 ---------- 50	49 ---------- 43	42 ---------- 27	26 ---------- 19	18 ---------- 14
2. Sensation Seeking (31–36 months)	/70	70 ---------- 59	58 ---------- 49	48 ---------- 28	27 ---------- 18	17 ---------- 14
3. Sensory Sensitivity (7–36 months)	38 /55	**	55 ---------- 53	52 ---------- 41	40 ---X--- 36	35 ---------- 11
4. Sensation Avoiding (7–36 months)	32 /60	**	60 ---------- 57	56 ---------- 45	44 ---------- 39	38 -X------ 12
Low Threshold	**Raw Score Total**	**Note:** This score is only relevant when both Quadrants 3 and 4 are outside the Typical Performance range.				
Low Threshold (7–36 months)	70 /115	**	115 ---------- 108	107 ---------- 87	86 ---------- 77	76 -X------ 23

*Classifications are based on the performance of children without disabilities ($n = 480$).
**There can be no Definite Difference for this section in this age range.

Figure 4.7 ■ **Completing the Quadrant Summary for a 14-Month-Old Child**

Completing the Sensory Processing Section Summary

The Sensory Processing Section Summary is located on page 4 of the *Summary Score Sheet* for children 7 to 36 months of age. There is no Sensory Processing Section Summary for children ages birth to 6 months because these scores were not stable for this age group. The Sensory Processing Section Summary provides a visual summary of the child's sensory processing abilities. Transfer the child's score for each section from the *Caregiver Questionnaire* to the corresponding column labeled Section Raw Score Total. Plot the child's section raw score totals by marking an X in the classification column that corresponds to the raw score total for each section.

Several sections have different cut scores depending on the child's age. Make sure you transfer the Section Raw Score Totals to the appropriate age band for each section (See Figure 4.8).

Sensory Processing Section Summary (7 to 36 Months)

Instructions: Transfer the Section Raw Score Totals from the 7 to 36 months Caregiver Questionnaire to the corresponding Section Raw Score Total box for the appropriate ages. Plot these totals by marking an X in the appropriate classification column (Typical Performance, Probable Difference, Definite Difference)*.

Sensory Processing Section	Section Raw Score Total	Less Than Others ←			→ More Than Others	
		Definite Difference	Probable Difference	Typical Performance	Probable Difference	Definite Difference
A. General Processing	No section raw score total is calculated for the General Processing Section.					
B. Auditory Processing (7–36 months)	45 /50	50 -------- 48	47 -------X 44	43 ---------- 35	34 ---------- 31	30 ---------- 10
C. Visual Processing (7–36 months)	23 /35	35--------- 32	31 ---------- 28	27 ---X--- 20	19 ---------- 16	15 ---------- 7
D. Tactile Processing (7–24 months)	/75	75 -------- 68	67 ---------- 62	61 ---------- 48	47 ---------- 42	41 ---------- 15
D. Tactile Processing (25–36 months)	42 /75	75--------- 72	71 ---------- 65	64 ---------- 51	50 ---------- 44	43 X-------- 15
E. Vestibular Processing (7–36 months)	20 /30	30--------- 27	26 ---------- 24	23 -----X--- 18	17 ---------- 15	14 ---------- 6
F. Oral Sensory Processing (7–12 months)	/35	35--------- 33	32 ---------- 30	29 ---------- 21	20 ---------- 17	16 ---------- 7
F. Oral Sensory Processing (13–18 months)	/35	**	35 ---------- 32	31 ---------- 23	22 ---------- 19	18 ---------- 7
F. Oral Sensory Processing (19–24 months)	/35	**	35 ---------- 33	32 ---------- 24	23 ---------- 20	19 ---------- 7
F. Oral Sensory Processing (25–30 months)	31 /35	**	35 ---------- 33	32 X-------- 25	24 ---------- 22	21 ---------- 7
F. Oral Sensory Processing (31–36 months)	/35	**	35 ---------- 34	33 ---------- 25	24 ---------- 21	20 ---------- 7

*Classifications are based on the performance of children without disabilities ($n = 489$)
**There can be no Definite Difference for this section in this age range.

Note: Reproducible Growth Curves for Children 7 to 36 months, for Sensation Seeking, Tactile Processing, and Oral Sensory Processing, are available in Appendix A of the *Infant/Toddler Sensory Profile User's Manual.*

Figure 4.8 ■ **Completing the Sensory Processing Section Summary for a 25-Month-Old Child**

CHAPTER 5

Interpretation

This chapter provides insights into interpretation of a child's performance on the *Infant/Toddler Sensory Profile* so that you can design more effective intervention strategies. The *Summary Score Sheet* was designed to simplify the scoring process, to facilitate comparisons of a child's performance to a sample of children without disabilities ($N = 589$), and to enable you to consider the performance differences across disability groups to make further interpretations. When combined with other data (other formal tests, observations, reports, referral concerns), you will be able to make decisions about the meaning of the child's performance in daily life using the *Infant/Toddler Sensory Profile* scores.

Using the Classification System for Interpretation

The *Infant/Toddler Sensory Profile* enables you to communicate a child's sensory processing abilities to parents and teachers as a profile of scores. It uses a classification system to organize the possible scores into one of two groups for children ages birth to 6 months and into one of three groups for children ages 7 to 36 months, based on the performance of the sample of children without disabilities ($N = 589$). The classification system's cut scores are provided on the *Summary Score Sheet* to aid in your interpretation process.

Classification System

Cut scores for children ages birth to 6 months were determined for each quadrant in the following manner (See Figure 5.1 for a graphic representation of the classification system for children ages birth to 6 months.):

- **Consult and Follow-up** corresponds to scores outside the + or –1 *SD* score for children without disabilities. Remember: infants can be more responsive (have lower scores) or less responsive (have higher scores) than peers. Therefore, there is a cut score at both ends of the continuum, corresponding to below –1 *SD* from the mean and above +1 *SD* from the mean respectively.
- **Typical Performance** corresponds to scores at or between + or –1 *SD* from the mean for children without disabilities.

Cut scores for children ages 7 to 36 months were determined for each section and quadrant in the following manner (See Figure 5.2 for a graphic representation of the classification system for children ages 7 to 36 months.):

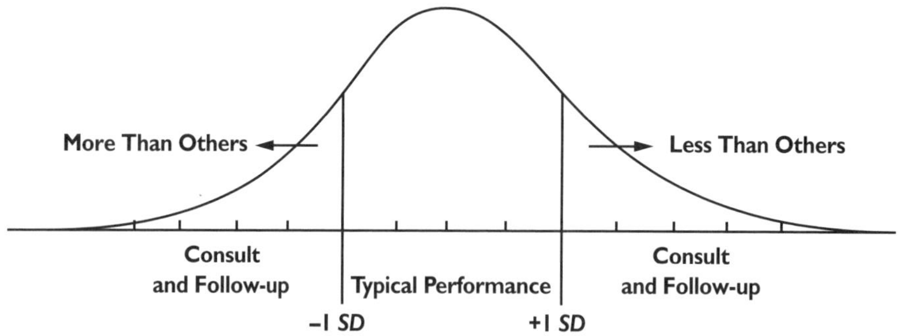

Figure 5.1 ■ **The Normal Curve and the *Infant/Toddler Sensory Profile* Classification System for Children Ages Birth to 6 Months**

- **Definite Difference** corresponds to scores outside + or –2 *SD* from the mean for children without disabilities.
  - Scores above the point 2 *SD* above the mean represent **underresponsiveness** when compared to peers.
  - Scores below the point 2 *SD* below the mean represent **overresponsiveness** when compared to peers.
- **Probable Difference** corresponds to scores within the 1 to 2 *SD* range; specifically:
  - Scores at or below the point 2 *SD* above the mean, but higher than 1 *SD* above the mean, for children without disabilities represent **underresponsiveness**.
  - Scores at or above the point 2 *SD* below the mean, but lower than 1 *SD* below the mean, for children without disabilities represent **overresponsiveness**.
- **Typical Performance** corresponds to scores at or between + or –1 *SD* from the mean for children without disabilities.

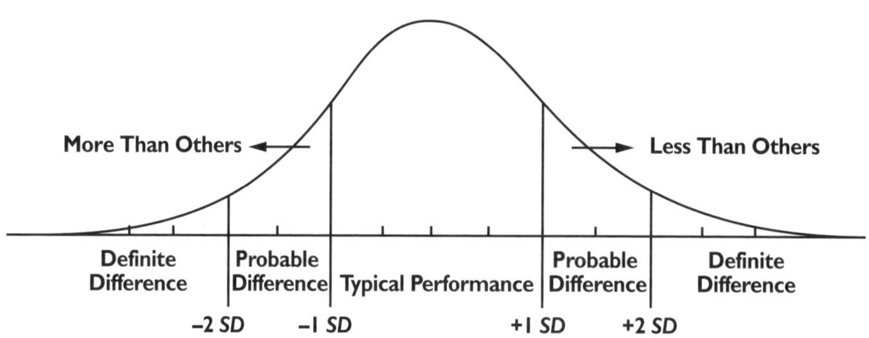

Figure 5.2 ■ **The Normal Curve and the *Infant/Toddler Sensory Profile* Classification System for Children Ages 7 to 36 Months**

Analysis of Demographic Variables

Researchers evaluated the effect of several demographic variables on the selected sample of children birth to 6 months of age and 7 to 36 months of age to determine whether professionals need to adjust their impressions when these characteristics are present. Multivariate Analysis of Variance was used to identify any possible differences among groups, obtaining the following results.

Weeks of Gestation

There were some significant differences in the data for children birth to 6 months of age. Seventy-five babies born at 40 weeks gestation and eleven babies born with less than 40 weeks gestation were included in the standardization sample (see Table 5.1). This distribution is insufficient to make firm conclusions, but the trend observed is interesting to note. The data reflect a trend in which babies born sooner than 38 weeks gestation had more frequent Low Threshold responses (Sensory Sensitivity, $p = .021$; Sensation Avoiding, $p = .001$). These results suggest that we can expect these babies to be hyperresponsive to stimuli during early months of development.

There were no significant differences in the data for children 7 to 36 months of age based on the time they were born in relation to their gestation. Because there was no significance in the larger data set for children ages 7 to 36 months, we might hypothesize that the effects of prematurity fade as the child gains more experience with sensation.

Table 5.1

Sample by Gestational Age

0–6 months *n*	Gestational Age	7–36 months *n*
75	40 weeks	333
11	Less than 40 weeks	40

Birth Order

Parents were asked to indicate the child's birth order in the family (see Table 5.2 for distribution). Although this variable was not significant for children ages birth to 6 months and children ages 7 to 36 months, there was an interesting trend in the data for the birth to 6-month-old age group (first born, $n = 28$; second born, $n = 29$; third born, $n = 19$; past third born, $n = 9$). The earlier the child was in the birth order the higher the parents rated Sensation Seeking behaviors. The Sensation Seeking scores for children in the fourth or later position in the family were more than 5 raw score points higher (i.e., less seeking) than children in earlier birth order positions.

Mean scores jumped more than 5 raw score points (toward less seeking) after the third birth order position. There are several possible reasons for this occurrence. Perhaps with 4 or more children, parents are less attentive to seeking behaviors. Another possibility is that babies in larger families exhibit more seeking behaviors with siblings than parents. A third possibility is that the context of a large family is so stimulating that the baby does not have to put forth the effort to seek stimuli as babies in smaller families do. In any case, this effect is no longer present in children 7 to 36 months, suggesting that as babies grow, there is an equalization of the impact of birth order.

Table 5.2

Sample by Birth Order

0–6 months *n*	Birth Order	7–36 months *n*
28	1st born	157
29	2nd born	138
19	3rd born	57
9	Past 3rd born	18

Number of Children in the Household

Number of children living in the household is frequently but not always related to birth order (See Table 5.3). In both the birth to 6 months of age and 7 to 36 months of age study groups, there is a significant difference in the Sensation Seeking score, with children in families with more than 3 children in the house having a lower amount of seeking. One might make the same hypotheses here as made with birth order; that parents are not attending to seeking behaviors, children engage in seeking behaviors with siblings, and/or children in larger families get stimulation without expending effort.

It would be useful to make note of the number of children in a household during assessment, so that professionals can make careful judgments of the possible impact of this situation on the child's scores.

Table 5.3

Sample by Number of Children in Household

0–6 months *n*	Number of children in the home	7–36 months *n*
26	1	112
36	2	159
20	3	63
11	More than 3	28

Person Reporting Data on the Infant/Toddler Sensory Profile

There were no differences in children's scores based on who completed the questionnaire. Only 3 fathers completed the questionnaire for children birth to 6 months, and only 16 fathers completed the questionnaire for children 7 to 36 months, so the overall data is skewed toward the biological mothers as the most common reporters (81 mothers of children ages birth to 6 months and 341 mothers of children ages 7 to 36 months). There were a few other types of informants, including adoptive parents, foster parents and other family members (2 in the data for children birth to 6 months and 18 in the data for children 7 to 36 months). However, an interesting finding here was that fathers had more variability in scores than mothers.

Using the Theoretical Model of Sensory Processing for Interpretation

As discussed in Chapter 2, Dunn (1997a) proposed a theoretical model for sensory processing based on the child's neurological thresholds and behavioral response patterns. In this model, the neurological threshold continuum is illustrated on the vertical axis, and the behavioral response/self regulation continuum is illustrated on the horizontal axis (see Figure 2.1 on page 8).

Low thresholds (bottom) and high thresholds (top) anchor the neurological threshold continuum. With a low threshold, the nervous system responds frequently to stimuli because it does not take very much input to reach the threshold and activate the system. With high thresholds, the nervous system does not respond to stimuli because it takes a lot of input to reach the threshold; therefore the system is dormant much of the time. Functional performance relies on a balance of activation and inhibition so that the child can be alert to selected stimuli while screening out other stimuli.

The behavioral response/self-regulation continuum is anchored by acting passively (left) and actively (right) in relation to one's thresholds (see Figure 2.1). When children act in a more passive way to stimuli they are responding in accordance with thresholds. When children actively respond to stimuli, they are counteracting their thresholds. These tendencies to respond are based on genetics, experience, and task and environmental demands.

These continua interact with each other to create four basic quadrants of responsivity (Low Registration, Sensation Seeking, Sensory Sensitivity, and Sensation Avoiding). It is important to keep in mind that:

1. Every person has some amount of each of these responsiveness characteristics. Someone may have Sensory Sensitivity to touch and be Sensation Seeking for sounds. One quadrant may seem to dominate a person's way of conducting daily life, but the other responsiveness patterns can still be present to a certain degree.
2. If a child has behaviors consistent with one of these quadrants, by itself that does not constitute a reason for concluding that the child is dysfunctional. When a child has performance difficulties in daily life, behaviors consistent with these quadrants can shed light on possible reasons for the child's difficulty and ways to address the performance problem.
3. Children can exhibit any combination of these patterns of behaviors, and the patterns can coexist because they represent various forms of modulation.

Low Registration

General Features

Behavior consistent with Low Registration represents high neurological thresholds and a tendency to act passively in relation to those thresholds. Children who have low registration tend to appear uninterested and can have a flat or dull affect. Children with low registration have low energy levels and act as if they are overly tired all the time. The rationale for this, using the sensory processing model, is that the brain is not getting what it needs to generate responses, and the child's tendency to respond in accordance with high thresholds leads to an apathetic, self-absorbed appearance. It is hypothesized that children with low registration have inadequate neural activation to support sustained performance and therefore may miss salient cues in the context to support ongoing responsivity.

Intervention Planning

If a child is identified as having low registration, and this feature is determined to be interfering with daily life, focus intervention planning toward enhancing task features and contextual cues in the activities of interest. This increases the chance that the child's thresholds will be met and neural responses generated. You can do this by increasing the contrast of stimuli (e.g., placing a contrasting color on the child's table surface to make the food more noticeable) or by decreasing the predictability of routines (e.g., changing the morning routine, requiring the child to pay more attention to what is happening).

The overall goal is to make all experiences more concentrated with sensory information so there is more likelihood that the thresholds will be met and the child will be able to notice and respond to cues in the environment.

Sensory Sensitivity

General Features

Behavior consistent with Sensory Sensitivity represents low neurological thresholds and a tendency to act passively in relation to those thresholds. Children who have sensory sensitivity tend to be distractible and may display hyperactivity. They have a pattern of directing their attention to the latest stimulus that presents itself, which draws them away from whatever they are trying to accomplish. They might be cautious about proceeding in some situations because they missed something (while being distracted), or might become upset either by their own difficulties with tracking tasks or with others who are interrupting them. It can be hypothesized that children who have sensory sensitivity have overreactive neural systems that make them aware of every stimulus that becomes available, and these children do not have the commensurate ability to habituate to these stimuli.

Intervention Planning

It is important to understand the meaning of these distractible behaviors when planning interventions. Be careful about withholding stimuli from these children; they still need input to operate, but cannot tolerate the influx of random input because their mechanisms of habituation are underdeveloped. For this child, you must understand how the nervous system, particularly the sensory systems, operates to establish the balance of power. Each sensory system has a component that enables arousal and alerting, and another component that supports discriminatory skills and mapping of self and environment. Children with sensory sensitivity do not need any more arousal and alerting stimuli; this mechanism is already informing them of new stimuli too often. Therefore, discriminatory input that supports organized patterns of information to the brain without generating additional arousal should be provided. Discriminatory input includes firm touch-pressure on the surface of the skin (as opposed to light touch), linear patterns of movement (as opposed to angular movement such as spinning or bending over), and predictable patterns of visual and auditory cues (as opposed to unexpected stimuli). For example, finding a waist-high bookshelf for the child's supplies and books instead of having his or her items at floor level would reduce the angular movement input of bending down to get things out for play (Dunn, 1997b).

The overall goals are to provide the child with sensory experiences as part of ongoing performance that support the child to continue a task and to minimize the chances for the thresholds to be fired repeatedly.

Sensation Seeking

General Features

Behavior consistent with Sensation Seeking represents high neurological thresholds with a tendency to actively work to meet these thresholds. Children who are sensation seekers are active and continuously engaged in their environments. These children add sensory input to every experience in daily life. They make noises while working, fidget, rub or explore objects with their skin, chew on things, and wrap body parts around furniture or people as ways to increase input during tasks. They may appear excitable or seem to lack consideration for safety while playing. One might hypothesize that children who are sensation seekers have inadequate neural activation (as do those with low registration), but they are driven to meet their thresholds and so create opportunities to increase input to meet their high thresholds.

Intervention Planning

Begin intervention planning for these children with skilled observation. Because these children create sensation for themselves, their behavior tells us what sensory input they need. Their performance problems are related to the interference of their seeking behaviors with ongoing performance, so the most effective strategy is to incorporate needed sensory input into daily routines. When caregivers can include the sensory input the children need while they are conducting their lives (e.g., during eating, personal hygiene, dressing), the children remain alert and don't have to interrupt their routines to load up on sensory input.

Be careful not to make the mistake of observing what the child likes related to sensory input and then using that as a reinforcer. For example, do not tell the child that when he or she accomplishes some learning task, the child can do whatever he or she craves. The theoretical model of sensory processing suggests that the child is demonstrating what he or she needs and you must provide it first to enable performance (i.e., as an antecedent), rather than make it contingent on performance.

Children who rock and fidget in their chairs need vestibular input; don't make them be still during a meal to earn playtime. They need to move about as a part of being ready and available for all activities. One way to provide vestibular input is to create rituals that require movement with purpose throughout the day (as opposed to running around randomly). For example, have the child carry toys to another room to put them away. This increases movement opportunities while also encouraging the child to keep attention to the task. Although this might be seen as a behavioral intervention, it is also a sensory one when you consider the body movement input available when moving about. You also could use a very malleable cushion on a high chair to provide ongoing movement input while the child is eating. The selection depends on the home setting, the family's needs, and the child's preferences.

The overall goal is to incorporate additional sensory input into the child's routines so that thresholds can be met while conducting daily life.

Sensation Avoiding

General Features

Behavior consistent with Sensation Avoiding represents low neurological thresholds with a tendency to actively work to keep these thresholds from being met. Children who are sensation avoiders might engage in very disruptive behaviors. It is hypothesized that meeting thresholds is uncomfortable or frightening to the child. In this case, the child's coping strategy is to keep these events at bay. Children do this by either withdrawing or engaging in an emotional outburst that enables them to get out of the threatening situation. Children who are sensation avoiders also might create rituals for their daily lives (hypothesized to be a strategy to allow only familiar patterns of input), and by their behavior entice others to support these rituals. For example, the child might have a good morning getting ready for an outing if his or her parent awakens the child a certain way, serves a certain breakfast food, and allows the child to wear certain clothing items. That same child might have a bad day if the ritual is altered. The parent learns what constitutes a good day and attempts to recreate it each day to facilitate getting the child ready for the day. From a behavioral perspective, this child might be stubborn or controlling. However, from a sensory processing perspective, the child is creating a situation to limit sensory input to those events that are familiar and therefore easy for the nervous system to interpret. Children who avoid sensation are resistant to changes because change represents an opportunity to be bombarded with unfamiliar (and, from an alerted nervous system's point of view, potentially harmful) stimuli.

Intervention Planning

The most important thing to remember when planning interventions for children who avoid sensation is to honor their need to reduce sensory input. There is something about unfamiliar input that generates sensitization, which interferes with ongoing performance. Forcing the child to get used to and to confront intense sensory input without systematic planning generates more defiant and withdrawing behaviors, making him or her even more unavailable for learning. These defiant behaviors must be understood as indications of the difficulty the child is having habituating, and a power struggle over this primal response to protect oneself must be avoided. This does not mean that you leave the child with the narrow range of acceptable input. Rather, you must carefully construct events to introduce a wider range of sensory experiences so the child can develop habituation for them. One easy way to do this is to take one of the child's imbedded rituals and expand it in one sensory way at a time. For example with the morning routine ritual, the parent might mix two cereals together (with texture differences) and leave everything else the same. Then when the child has processed that as part of the ritual, the parent can change something else.

The overall goal is to honor the child's need to limit unfamiliar sensory input and gradually broaden the sensory processing experiences within the child's accepted rituals.

Low Threshold (Combined Quadrant)

General Features

Behavior consistent with Low Threshold (a combined score of the Sensory Sensitivity and Sensation Avoiding quadrants) represents low neurological thresholds with children using both active and passive self-regulation strategies. Children who have low thresholds tend to be fussy and require a great deal of structure. Parents and other care providers may report that these children are inconsistent. This apparent inconsistency reflects the nervous system's attempts to simultaneously respond to stimuli and protect itself by reducing input, therefore producing variable responses.

We included this combined score for two reasons. First, many of the disability groups exhibited both sensation avoiding and sensory sensitivity, suggesting a range of low threshold responding strategies. Second, in data analyses, items from these two quadrants frequently mixed together in factor analyses. The high threshold groups (sensation seeking and low registration) were much more discrete.

If one of the Low Threshold scores (Sensation Avoiding or Sensory Sensitivity) ends up in the Typical Performance range, the combined Low Threshold score will not be useful. This score is only relevant when both the Sensation Avoiding and Sensory Sensitivity quadrant scores are outside the Typical Performance range, as a means for characterizing a Low Threshold condition. Merging a Typical Performance score with a score outside the Typical Performance range will mask the pertinent contrast. In these cases, use the separate quadrant scores to interpret the child's performance, taking full advantage of the specific information provided by the quadrant scores.

Intervention Planning

When a child has low thresholds for responding, that child is likely to be overly vigilant and rigid. You can refer to the sections for Sensory Sensitivity and Sensation Avoiding for general guidance, but you must remember that when children have overall low threshold responding (rather than one or the other of the Low Threshold quadrants being different), the children are more likely to respond with variability from day to day or hour to hour, making it hard for parents and other care providers to plan or anticipate what will work.

The most important factor in intervention planning is providing information about the range of performance to be expected, from irritability to shutting down. It is helpful to solicit examples from the care providers about the specific child so they can begin to understand this apparent inconsistency. Sometimes it is also helpful to watch a video of the child with the care providers and talk about the behaviors, their functions, and their meanings before making recommendations. Once care providers begin to have insight, they will see patterns in performance, what triggers reactions, and what parameters keep the child functional.

Using Growth Charts to Make Further Interpretations

Three growth charts have been created to support your work as well. Unlike the *Sensory Profile*, in which scores are relatively stable across the 3 to 10 year age groups, the *Infant/Toddler Sensory Profile* shows some developmental trends in the data for children 7 to 36 months. Specifically, there are 3 scores that shifted during the infant/toddler period: Sensation Seeking, Tactile Processing, and Oral Sensory Processing. You will see on the score sheets that you must select the row corresponding to the child's age when recording the score.

We thought it might also be useful to create a graph illustrating this growth pattern (in every case as children grow older, they respond LESS FREQUENTLY to stimuli). Therefore, Appendix A contains reproducible graphs reflecting these developmental trends. The growth curves were designed similarly to other growth curves in which age is the horizontal axis and score is the vertical axis. Graph the child's score at the intersection between the score point and the age point.

The growth charts represent the same scores you record on the *Summary Score Sheet*. There are a pair of lines in the center that border the Typical Performance range, and 2 additional pairs of lines marking the Probable Difference and Definite Difference areas on the graph. **Remember: children can respond significantly MORE than others (lower scores) or significantly LESS than others (higher scores).**

Using Performance Differences Across Disability Groups to Make Further Interpretations

Therapists provided (see Acknowledgments) data on children with various disabilities in addition to the standardization sample. These data were analyzed to provide professionals with information regarding the performance of these groups for both validity analyses and to guide interpretation.

We compared children ages 7 to 36 months with disabilities to matched groups of children without disabilities in the following categories:

- Developmental delays ($n = 69$)
- Health impairments and metabolic disorders ($n = 29$)
- Pervasive developmental disorders, including autism ($n = 24$)
- Down syndrome ($n = 18$)
- Developmental delays and other diagnoses ($n = 18$)
- Sensory integrative dysfunction ($n = 12$)
- Language delays ($n = 8$)

We also compared 21 children ages birth to 6 months with reflux to a matched group of infants without disabilities.

To illustrate these relationships, we graphed the mean and –1 *SD* to +1 *SD* scores for children with and without disabilities. Appendix B displays these relationships; the X represents the mean for the groups, while the brackets represent –1 *SD* and +1 *SD* for each group.

Overall Trends Across Groups

This section summarizes trends between children with and without disabilities in the data.

Seeking is similar for everyone. In nearly all cases, sensation seeking is the same for children 7 to 36 months in all groups. Only the children with language delays had slight differences when compared to children without disabilities but this group is very small so this must be considered preliminary evidence. Sensation seeking is also one of the scores that is characterized by a developmental trend, with children ages 7 to 36 months engaging in more seeking behaviors as they grow older. Perhaps the developmental trend creates a broader range of acceptable performance, and therefore children with various disabilities have a better chance to obtain scores somewhere along this developmental continuum.

Preliminary evidence suggests that children in some disability groups may have typical sensory processing.

> **Children ages 7 to 36 months with Down syndrome may have typical sensory processing.** In our matched sample comparison, children ages 7 to 36 months with Down syndrome had scores comparable to their peers without disabilities. We need a larger sample to make conclusive statements. Perhaps sensory processing is not a core feature of Down syndrome. If this is true, other factors must create the interference to performance, and must be investigated.
>
> **Children ages 7 to 36 months with language delays may have typical sensory processing.** Toddlers with language delays also had scores comparable

to their matched peers. This group is very small and we would need a larger sample to make conclusive statements. It is likely that sensory processing is not a primary area of concern for this group of children either.

Low threshold scores are statistically significantly lower for children in several disability groups. When children ages 7 to 36 months have disabilities with a sensory processing feature, it is much more likely that Low Threshold scores (Sensory Sensitivity, Sensation Avoiding, and the combined Low Threshold score) will be low (i.e., children with disabilities engage in the behaviors more frequently than matched peers without disabilities). Perhaps a central feature of these developmental disabilities (autism, developmental delay, health impairments and metabolic disorders, sensory integrative dysfunction) involves the brain's difficulty with habituation to stimuli, with the result that stimuli continues to generate noticing and arousal for these children when others have stopped noticing stimuli.

Only some disability groups have difficulty with Low Registration. Only children ages 7 to 36 months with developmental delays, autism, and sensory integrative disorders had lower scores on Low Registration (i.e., they fail to notice stimuli more often). These groups also had low Low Threshold scores (i.e., they were more sensitive and/or withdrew from stimuli they noticed more often). Perhaps the presence of low thresholds and low registration indicates poor modulation. That is, these children may not notice stimuli they need to notice, but when they notice stimuli, their nervous systems have intolerance for input. This creates a difficult situation, one in which there is a very small range for processing sensory information for use in performance in daily life.

Note: Remember that frequent behaviors receive lower scores; therefore, children get lower scores for engaging in behaviors more frequently and higher scores for engaging in behaviors less frequently.

Performance Differences for Particular Disability Groups

We conducted a series of studies to determine the usefulness of the *Infant/Toddler Sensory Profile* for identifying differences in special populations. Generally, the *Infant/Toddler Sensory Profile* discriminates between children with and without disabilities, with the children with various disabilities engaging in the behaviors more often (i.e., had lower scores) than the children without disabilities.

For each study reported below, children with disabilities were each paired with a child from the sample without disabilities. The children in the studies were matched by age, gender, socioeconomic status, ethnic origin, and community size.

Multivariate Analysis of Variance (MANOVA) was used to test whether the children with disabilities performed differently from children without disabilities on the *Infant/Toddler Sensory Profile.*

Performance of Children With Developmental Delays (n = 69)

This study included children with developmental delays and a matched sample of children without disabilities. Table 5.4 contains a summary of the demographic variables of the matched sample.

Children with developmental delays had statistically significantly lower scores (i.e., engaged in behaviors more frequently) than their matched peers on 9 of 10 possible scores. The sample size provided over 99% power to detect a large effect size. The observed effect sizes (reported as eta squared) indicate that these differences are noticeable and relevant for practice. Table 5.5 contains a summary of the data from these comparisons, and Appendix B illustrates group pattern differences in a series of graphs.

Table 5.4

Demographic Information for Matched Sample of Children With and Without Disabilities

Note: first number is disability group/second number is matched group without disabilities

Demographics of children with/without disabilities	Developmental delays* ($n = 69$)	Health impairments and metabolic disorders* ($n = 29$)	Pervasive developmental disorders, including autism* ($n = 24$)	Down syndrome* ($n = 18$)	Developmental delay and other diagnoses* ($n = 18$)	Sensory integrative disfunction* ($n = 12$)	Language delays* ($n = 8$)	Cerebral palsy* ($n = 8$)	Reflux* ($n = 21$)
Gender**									
Male	43/44	16/16	20/20	11/11	12/12	9/9	6/6	6/6	12/12
Female	25/25	13/13	4/4	7/7	6/6	3/3	2/2	2/2	9/9
Age groups in months**									
Birth to 6	0/0	0/0	0/0	0/0	0/0	0/0	0/0	0/0	21/21
7 to 12	9/9	4/4	0/0	2/2	3/3	0/0	0/0	1/1	0/0
13 to 24	30/30	13/13	2/2	7/7	9/8	2/2	3/3	3/2	0/0
25 to 36	30/30	12/12	22/22	9/9	6/7	10/10	5/5	4/5	0/0
Region**									
Northeast	21/17	7/9	16/11	10/1	6/6	4/2	1/2	3/1	4/2
North Central	24/26	12/10	5/4	4/8	4/5	1/5	2/1	5/3	3/9
South	18/6	6/5	0/3	2/1	4/2	0/0	3/3	0/2	1/3
West	6/17	3/5	1/5	2/8	4/4	6/5	2/1	0/1	0/7
Ethnicity**									
Native	2/0	0/0	0/0	1/0	0/0	0/0	0/0	0/0	0/0
Asian	1/0	0/0	0/2	0/0	0/0	0/0	0/0	0/0	0/0
African American	3/2	5/2	0/0	0/0	0/1	0/0	1/0	0/0	1/1
Latino	3/1	3/2	0/2	0/0	1/0	0/0	0/1	0/0	0/0
Caucasian	51/64	19/25	20/20	12/17	16/15	10/9	7/7	7/8	19/18
Other	9/2	2/0	2/0	5/1	1/2	2/3	0/0	1/0	1/2

*For each disability group, the samples of children are matched by gender and age, and to the extent possible, by ethnicity, community, and yearly income.

**When the data does not add up to *n*, it means the families did not provide the information.

Table 5.5

MANOVA of Matched Sample Comparison of Children Who Have Developmental Delay and Children Without Disabilities (*n* = 69 in each group)

	F	Significance	Effect Size (Eta squared)
Low Registration	27.199	<.001****	.234
Sensation Seeking	2.978	.088	.032
Sensory Sensitivity	15.603	<.001****	.149
Sensation Avoiding	15.946	<.001****	.152
Low Threshold	15.123	<.001****	.130
Auditory Processing	15.173	<.001****	.146
Visual Processing	25.853	<.001****	.225
Tactile Processing	7.801	.006**	.081
Vestibular Processing	13.651	<.001****	.133
Oral Sensory Processing	23.162	<.001****	.207

*p < .05
**p < .01
***p < .005
****p < .001

These data indicate that professionals can use the *Infant/Toddler Sensory Profile* as part of overall assessment, and that these data could be helpful in directing intervention planning to include sensory processing features. It is interesting that the Sensation Seeking score is the same for both groups; this is the one quadrant score that shows a developmental trend, rather than being stable across ages. Perhaps children in this category are developing their seeking strategies in similar ways to their peers. This would be a positive feature to point out to families and other care providers.

Performance of Children With Health Impairments and Metabolic Disorders (*n* = 29)

This study included children with other diagnoses of young childhood, including allergies, asthma, fetal alcohol syndrome, heart conditions, and sensory impairments, and a matched sample of children without disabilities. Table 5.4 contains a summary of the demographic variables of the matched sample.

Children with health impairments and metabolic disorders had statistically significantly lower scores (i.e., engaged in behaviors more frequently) than their matched peers on 6 of 10 possible scores. The sample size provided over 87% power to detect a large effect size. The observed effect sizes (reported as eta squared) indicate that these differences are noticeable and relevant for practice. Table 5.6 contains a summary of the data from these comparisons, and Appendix B illustrates group pattern differences in a series of graphs.

In relation to the quadrant scores, this group of children scores the same as comparison children on high threshold items (Sensation Seeking and Low Registration) and significantly lower than peers on low threshold items (Sensory Sensitivity and

Table 5.6

MANOVA of Matched Sample Comparison of Children Who Have Health Impairments and Metabolic Disorders and Children Without Disabilities (n = 29 in each group)

	F	Significance	Effect Size (Eta squared)
Low Registration	1.842	.186	.066
Sensation Seeking	.476	.486	.018
Sensory Sensitivity	18.801	<.001****	.420
Sensation Avoiding	8.549	.007**	.247
Low Threshold	8.063	.007**	.175
Auditory Processing	.848	.365	.032
Visual Processing	6.567	.017*	.202
Tactile Processing	13.754	.001**	.346
Vestibular Processing	5.326	.029*	.170
Oral Sensory Processing	2.974	.096	.103

*$p < .05$
**$p < .01$
***$p < .005$
****$p < .001$

Sensation Avoiding). Perhaps the various disorders have some association with heightened responsiveness, and the *Infant/Toddler Sensory Profile* provides a tool for recording this aspect of the conditions.

It is unclear why visual, tactile and vestibular sections would be significant while auditory and oral sensory areas were not. We will need further study of these groups of children to understand this pattern.

Performance of Children With Pervasive Developmental Disorders Including Autism (n = 24)

This study included children with pervasive developmental disorders and a matched sample of children without disabilities. Table 5.4 contains a summary of the demographic variables of the matched sample.

Children with autism and other pervasive developmental disorders had statistically significantly lower scores (i.e., engaged in behaviors more frequently) than their matched peers on 9 of 10 possible scores. The sample size provided over 78% power to detect a large effect size. The observed effect sizes (reported as eta squared) indicate that these differences are noticeable and relevant for practice. Table 5.7 contains a summary of the data from these comparisons, and Appendix B illustrates group pattern differences in a series of graphs.

As with the *Sensory Profile* for children, (see Kientz & Dunn, 1997; Ermer & Dunn, 1998) the *Infant/Toddler Sensory Profile* seems to be measuring a feature of interest when assessing children with autism and other pervasive developmental disorders. In every case, the children with autism engaged in the behaviors indicated more frequently than their matched peers.

Table 5.7

MANOVA of Matched Sample Comparison of Children Who Have Pervasive Developmental Disorders, Including Autism and Children Without Disabilities (n = 24 in each group)

	F	Significance	Effect Size (Eta squared)
Low Registration	43.399	<.001****	.583
Sensation Seeking	.017	.897	.001
Sensory Sensitivity	32.395	<.001****	.511
Sensation Avoiding	53.227	<.001****	.632
Low Threshold	42.024	<.001****	.539
Auditory Processing	31.546	<.001****	.504
Visual Processing	12.503	<.001****	.287
Tactile Processing	19.657	<.001****	.388
Vestibular Processing	15.186	<.001****	.329
Oral Sensory Processing	32.832	<.001****	.514

*p < .05
**p < .01
***p < .005
****p < .001

It is interesting that the Sensation Seeking score is the same for both groups. Nonetheless, with this finding we need to reconsider the meaning of some of the high rate behaviors of children who have autism (e.g., rocking, hand flapping). Although on first consideration, these behaviors may seem to have a seeking function, these findings suggest that is not the case. Perhaps these behaviors serve the purpose of keeping unfamiliar stimuli away, suggesting a sensation avoiding function. This would be a positive feature to point out to families and other care providers.

Performance of Children With Down Syndrome (*n* = 18)

This study included children with Down syndrome and a matched sample of children without disabilities. Table 5.4 contains a summary of the demographic variables of the matched sample.

The children with Down syndrome performed just like other children on all but one of the scores on the *Infant/Toddler Sensory Profile*. The only significantly lower score was in the Auditory Processing section (F = 4.61, significance = .043, eta squared = .180). The children with Down syndrome had scores indicating more frequent performance than peers.

This was a small sample, so we must be cautious in our conclusions and generalizations. It is interesting that in this sample, children with Down syndrome had nearly the same sensory processing patterns as their peers. It is possible that cognitive processing is a more primary concern for children with Down syndrome, and sensory processing is intact. Perhaps sensory processing does not need to be part of routine assessment for this group, and is only warranted if there are other factors that might suggest difficulty with sensory processing.

As part of a comprehensive assessment, the *Infant/Toddler Sensory Profile* may provide a way to demonstrate an area of typical performance for families and teachers who may only be hearing about areas of concern.

Performance of Children With Developmental Delays and Other Diagnoses (*n* = 18)

This study included children with developmental delays combined with another diagnosis (including those listed alone in the metabolic disorders and health conditions group), and a matched sample of children without disabilities. Table 5.4 contains a summary of the demographic variables of the matched sample.

Children with developmental delays and other diagnoses had statistically significantly lower scores (i.e., engaged in behaviors more frequently) than their matched peers on 5 of 10 possible scores. The sample size provided over 66% power to detect a large effect size. The observed effect sizes (reported as eta squared) indicate that these differences are noticeable and relevant for practice.

The overall multivariate test for the quadrants was not significant, but the low threshold groupings were significant when tested separately.

It is unclear why children with a combination of developmental delay and other conditions would have more typical scores than either the developmental delay or the 'other' diagnoses groups alone. However, this preliminary finding suggests that professionals need to be cautious about presuming that children with coexisting conditions will demonstrate the same pattern of scores as children with only one of those conditions.

Performance of Children With Sensory Integrative Dysfunction (*n* = 12)

This study included children identified as having sensory integrative dysfunction by the therapists serving their families and a matched sample of children without disabilities. Table 5.4 contains a summary of the demographic variables of the matched sample.

Children with sensory integrative dysfunction had statistically significantly lower scores (i.e., engaged in behaviors more frequently) than their matched peers on all of the quadrant scores. The sample size provided only 47% power to detect a large effect size. The overall multivariate test for the sections (i.e., the sensory system scores) was not significant, but 4 of the 5 section scores were significant when tested separately.

In earlier studies, McIntosh, Miller, Shyu, & Dunn (1999) demonstrated that children with sensory modulation disorder performed significantly differently than typically developing peers on the *Sensory Profile* and the *Short Sensory Profile*. These data indicate that, even with the small sample of children, the *Infant/Toddler Sensory Profile* can also identify the unique sensory processing patterns of this group of children. This preliminary evidence supports using the *Infant/Toddler Sensory Profile* in early assessment protocols.

Performance of Children With Language Delays (*n* = 8)

A small sample of children with language delays was also analyzed. Table 5.4 provides a summary of their demographic information.

Initial Multivariate Analyses of Variance indicated that there were no differences overall in either the quadrant or section scores (analyses were run on these separately to ensure no duplication of data). However, the follow up univariate tests revealed that the Sensation Seeking quadrant and the Visual Processing section scores were significantly lower than their matched peer group. In both cases, the children with language disorders engaged in the behaviors more frequently.

These two differences were unexpected, and it would be inappropriate to make statements based on 8 children. What can be said is that children with language delays may perform like their peers in most sensory processing. Again, as part of comprehensive assessment, showing areas of typical performance both informs parents of strengths to build on and provides clarity about the discrete nature of the child's areas of need. Larger samples are needed to make any conclusions.

Performance of Children With Cerebral Palsy (*n* = 8)

Eight children with cerebral palsy were included in our data set, but only 2 of them had complete data for analysis. Table 5.4 provides a summary of their demographic information.

The fact that most parents of these children were unable to complete the *Infant/Toddler Sensory Profile* suggests that there are other factors that need to be investigated before we can make statements about their patterns of sensory processing. Additionally, incomplete forms for this group when other groups were able to provide complete data suggests that other factors may be more critical to address during the early years.

Performance of Infants With Reflux (*n* = 21)

This study included children birth to 6 months identified as having reflux by the team serving their families, and a matched sample of children without disabilities. Table 5.4 contains a summary of the demographic variables of the matched sample.

Infants with reflux had statistically significantly lower scores (i.e., engaged in behaviors more frequently) than their matched peers in the Sensory Sensitivity quadrant, which is a low threshold set of response items. The sample size provided over 73% power to detect a large effect size. The observed effect sizes (reported as eta squared) indicate that these differences are noticeable and relevant for practice. Table 5.8 contains a summary of the data from these comparisons, and Appendix B illustrates group pattern differences in a series of graphs.

Table 5.8

Analysis of Performance of Infants With Reflux (*n* = 21 in each group)

	F	Significance	Effect Size (Eta squared)
Low Registration	.006	.937	<.001
Sensation Seeking	.475	.496	.016
Sensory Sensitivity	9.444	.005**	.246
Sensation Avoiding	.960	.335	.032
Low Threshold	10.181	.003***	.221

**p < .01
***p < .005

Although sensory section scores are not part of the infant scoring system, we conducted an analysis of the sensory systems for this group of infants. The Vestibular and General Sensory sections were significantly different from the peer group and contributed to the low Sensory Sensitivity score.

The combination of Sensory Sensitivity, Vestibular, and General Sensory scores being significantly different for infants with reflux is consistent with skilled observations of these children being irritable. Perhaps the *Infant/Toddler Sensory Profile* provides a means for documenting these characteristics during comprehensive assessment.

Spanish Version Comparisons

A small sample of Spanish-speaking families responded to a translated version of the *Infant/Toddler Sensory Profile*. Children were matched by age and gender with English-speaking children from the national sample to make a comparison of language effects (n = 29). The sample size provided over 89% power to detect a large effect size. Demographic data for the Spanish sample is summarized in Table 5.9.

Table 5.9

Demographics for Matched Sample for Spanish Version

	Demographics	***n* = 29***
Gender	Male	11
	Female	16
Age groups in months	Birth–6	2
	7–12	9
	13–24	4
	25–36	14
Region	Northeast	0
	North central	0
	South	16
	West	0
Ethnicity	Native American	0
	Asian	1
	African American	2
	Latino	22
	Caucasian	1
	Other	2

*When the data does not add up to *n*, it means the families did not provide the information.

Two Multivariate Analyses of Variance (MANOVA) were conducted using these data. First, researchers evaluated possible differences in the quadrant scores (Low Registration, Sensation Seeking, Sensory Sensitivity, and Sensation Avoiding). The MANOVA was not significant (Hotellings T significance = .152; eta squared = .236).

Secondly, researchers evaluated possible differences in the sensory processing scores (Auditory, Visual, Tactile, Vestibular, and Oral Sensory). The MANOVA for this analysis was significant (Hotellings T significance = .028; eta squared = .391). Follow up analyses revealed that the only sensory processing section that was significant was the Auditory Processing section.

With this result, researchers wanted to identify what items might be accounting for the significant difference, so a MANOVA was conducted using only the Auditory Processing items. The resulting overall MANOVA (n = 24) was not significant (Hotellings T significance = .094; eta squared = .342). Although this overall test would not lead researchers to look any further, in this case researchers did examine the follow up tests on individual auditory items. There were 2 of 10 auditory items that met statistical significance; the confidence intervals overlap very little, illustrating the differences, with Spanish speaking children less likely to engage in these two behaviors. Table 5.10 summarizes these findings.

Table 5.10

Summary of Analysis of Spanish Data

Items on the 7 to 36 month old version	Significance	Effect size (Eta squared)	Means (*SD*) of groups	Mean difference
Item #6 My child enjoys making sounds with his/her mouth.	.015	.126	English: 1.72(.245) Spanish: 2.58(.235)	0.86*
Item #10 My child ignores me when I am talking.	.006	.157	English: 4.0(.168) Spanish: 4.66(.161)	0.66*

*Higher scores mean the child engages in less of the behaviors [Almost Never = 5; Almost Always = 1]. Therefore, children in Spanish-speaking homes engage in these behaviors a little less than matched peers from English-speaking homes.

The results of this study indicated that it is probably reasonable in most cases to use the English cut scores when administering the Spanish version, although you must use your clinical judgment when doing so. Because of the small sample size (n = 29), proceed cautiously when interpreting differences on the Spanish version, especially when considering Auditory Processing items #6 "My child enjoys making sounds with his/her mouth" and #10 "My child ignores me when I am talking."

Due to the small sample sizes used in this study, be careful in drawing conclusions about the comparisons between the Spanish and English version of the *Infant/Toddler Sensory Profile*. It is promising that almost all of the items showed no significant differences, but further research with larger sample sizes is needed. Future work needs to include further analysis of the effects of culture and language and evaluation of the performance of infants birth to 6 months since they were not included in this study.

CHAPTER 6

Evidence Base for Reliability and Validity

Introduction to the Technical Aspects of the *Infant/Toddler Sensory Profile*

Good assessments yield "good" scores. Test developers demonstrate that an assessment is good by providing evidence for reliability and validity. The terms reliability and validity are central to your understanding of tests and testing. Yet the meaning of these terms continues to evolve and is not well understood by all test users (AERA, 1999). This chapter will provide a better understanding of the concepts of reliability and validity, and in particular what they mean when using the *Infant/Toddler Sensory Profile*.

Reliability and Errors of Measurement

Reliability refers to the consistency of scores obtained under the theoretical concept of repeated testing of the same individual on the same test under identical conditions (including no changes to the individual). This could never be done, and various estimates of reliability are obtained in practice.

There are two basic types of estimates for reliability. One is called test-retest reliability. Here, the individual is given the same test twice, under as similar conditions as possible. The individual will obviously not be identical at the two testings. However, the interval between test and retest is chosen to be as small as possible to minimize changes in the individual, yet long enough that any practice or memory effects have dissipated. In practice, we are usually only concerned with changes in the individual that are directly related to the construct being measured.

The second type of estimated reliability is internal consistency. Here we avoid any changes in the individual by administering only a single test. In one procedure the test is broken into two halves, which are then correlated with each other. A correction for the shortened length of these tests is then applied. To the degree that the halves are comparable, and each represents the whole test, this is a good estimate of the reliability. Rather than selecting a single split-half, we calculated a coefficient alpha which is the average of all possible split-halves.

Note also that both test-retest reliability and internal consistency provide not only an estimate of the theoretical concept of reliability, but also direct measures of test stability for repeated testing, and unidimensionality of the test, respectively.

A concept related to test reliability is the standard error of measurement (SEM). Reliability describes the theoretical consistency of the test for a group of test-takers, and can be used to calculate the SEM, which provides a measure of the accuracy of the test score for an individual. It provides information on how close the observed test score is likely to be to the person's true score, and can be used to place confidence intervals about the person's score (a range of scores within which the person's true score is likely to fall).

Therefore, the reliability of this test must be estimated. Two methods were used to estimate the reliability of the *Infant/Toddler Sensory Profile*: internal consistency (coefficient alpha), and test-retest reliability.

Evidence of Internal Consistency

Internal consistency estimates of reliability provide information about the consistency of responses to all items on a scale or subscale or, as in the *Infant/Toddler Sensory Profile*, for each sensory processing and quadrant grouping. Internal consistency coefficients help to evaluate how homogenous the item responses are within a scale. Coefficient alpha is an index of internal consistency ranging from 0 (no consistency) to 1 (perfect consistency). Coefficient alpha was calculated to examine the internal consistency for each sensory processing and quadrant grouping of the *Infant/Toddler Sensory Profile*. The values of alpha for the various groupings of items for children ages 7 to 36 months ranged from .42 to .86 as shown in Table 6.1. The values of alpha for the various groupings of items for children ages birth to 6 months ranged from .17 to .83 as shown in Table 6.1. You will note the sensory processing sections for children ages birth to 6 months have low alpha coefficients, suggesting poor overall consistency; therefore we do not provide section scores for these children.

Table 6.1

Coefficient Alpha

	Coefficient Alpha	
Sensory Processing Sections	**Children birth to 6 months**	**Children 7 to 36 months**
General Processing	.2684*	.6310
Auditory Processing	.4316*	.6961
Visual Processing	.4041*	.5453
Tactile Processing	.5723*	.7149
Vestibular Processing	.1670*	.4234
Oral Sensory Processing	N/A	.5518
Quadrants		
Low Registration	.6164	.6997
Sensation Seeking	.7869	.8580
Sensory Sensitivity	.7893	.7165
Sensation Avoiding	.5600	.6970
Combined Quadrant		
Low Threshold	.8283	.8307

*Due to the overall low coefficients in this group, these scores are not reliable; therefore they are not part of the final scoring system.

Evidence of Test-Retest Reliability

Obtaining ratings of the same child's sensory processing abilities from the same person at two different times provides both an estimate of the person's reliability and information on the stability of those ratings across multiple evaluations. A caregiver's view of a child can vary from time to time, but there must be some measurement consistency over time if the rating scales are to be useful for decision-making. Test-retest reliability coefficients will be at their highest when the child's target sensory processing ability is relatively stable across time and the respondent rates the child under similar conditions on both occasions. Test-retest reliability of the *Infant/Toddler Sensory Profile* was measured by having a subsample of the caregivers in the standardization sample (n = 32) rate their child 2 to 3 weeks after their initial rating for standardization purposes. The sample consisted of 32 children who were between the ages of 7 and 36 months. The sample was 47% female and 53% male. The racial/ethnic representation was 81% White, 10% African American, 3% Asian and 6% reported more than one ethnic background. The regional representation was 31% Northeast, 50% North Central, 16% South and 3% West.

The test-retest correlation coefficient for these data was .86 for the sensory processing section scores and .74 for the quadrant scores.

These coefficients indicate that the *Infant/Toddler Sensory Profile* caregiver rating is somewhat stable over time and is acceptable for the purposes of identification of target areas for intervention.

Standard Error of Measurement

Reliability coefficients are useful for evaluating a test's consistency of measurement for a group of children, but are not directly applicable to the interpretation of individual test scores. For a single score, the standard error of measurement (SEM) indicates the variability expected in obtained scores around the "true" score. In other words, error of measurement indicates how much a child's score might vary if the child were repeatedly rated on the same instrument under identical situations. In practice, most children will be rated once on the *Infant/Toddler Sensory Profile* prior to intervention implementation. The resulting score for the child is an estimate of his or her true score that includes some error. Thus, the SEM of a test helps users gain a sense of how much the child's score is likely to differ from his or her true score.

The more reliable a test is, the smaller the standard error of measurement (SEM) and the smaller the confidence intervals around a test score. Measurement error can occur for a variety of reasons (e.g., caregivers guessing or recording responses incorrectly, examiners giving misinformation, miscalculation of scores, unclear directions or items).

The standard error of measurement is an index of the degree to which obtained scores differ from true scores. The *Infant/Toddler Sensory Profile* provides a standard error of measurement value for each possible section and quadrant raw score total for each cut score group (see Table 6.2).

As seen in Table 6.2, the SEMs on the *Infant/Toddler Sensory Profile* for children ages birth to 6 months range from 1.41 to 3.77 raw score points on the quadrants. The SEMs for children 7 to 36 months range from 1.91 to 4.52 on the quadrants and from 1.85 to 3.66 on the sections. The SEMs for both the samples of children birth to 6 months and 7 to 36 months indicate small to moderate reliability, suggesting consistency can be expected from the *Infant/Toddler Sensory Profile*.

Table 6.2
Standard Error of Measurement

	SEM						
	Birth to 3 months	**4 to 6 months**	**7 to 12 months**	**13 to 18 months**	**19 to 24 months**	**25 to 30 months**	**31 to 36 months**
Sensory Processing Sections							
General Processing	N/A	N/A	N/A	N/A	N/A	N/A	N/A
Auditory Processing	N/A	N/A	1.93	1.96	2.47	2.27	2.95
Visual Processing	N/A	N/A	2.22	2.29	2.62	2.16	2.65
Tactile Processing	N/A	N/A	3.28	3.26	3.64	3.32	3.66
Vestibular Processing	N/A	N/A	2.11	1.85	2.20	1.86	2.16
Oral Sensory Processing	N/A	N/A	3.22	3.23	3.13	2.72	3.23
Quadrants							
Low Registration	3.07	2.84	2.12	2.07	2.15	1.91	2.30
Sensation Seeking	1.99	1.41	3.01	3.10	3.25	2.85	4.11
Sensory Sensitivity	2.38	3.11	2.72	2.48	2.70	2.91	3.22
Sensation Avoiding	1.70	2.00	3.04	2.92	2.98	3.14	3.14
Combined Quadrant							
Low Threshold	2.85	3.77	4.05	3.81	4.07	4.26	4.52

Note: These SEMs were calculated using alphas from Table 6.1 and standard deviations (*SD*) from Table 3.11 and 3.12.

Calculating Confidence Intervals

A confidence interval is a range of scores within which you can be highly confident that the child's true score actually lies. For example, if you calculate the 95% confidence interval, you can be 95% confident that the child's true score is within this interval.

Confidence intervals are developed assuming the data follows a normal curve. Because 95% of scores under a normal curve are within 1.96 standard deviations *(SD)* of the mean, a 95% confidence interval is found by adding and subtracting 1.96 times the number of standard deviations from the score. To develop a 95% confidence interval for a particular score, the standard deviation of the sample distribution is the standard error of measurement; therefore, the appropriate standard deviation is the standard error of measurement. Therefore, the confidence interval becomes the score +/- 1.96 x SEM.

Note that for very high or very low raw scores it is possible that the confidence interval will fall outside the range of possible obtained scores. However, this is not a problem because the confidence interval is for the true score.

Example of calculating a confidence interval for a 10 month old

Justin's section raw score total for Section B. Auditory Processing = 30

SEM for this score = 1.93 (see Table 6.2)

1.96 x 1.93 = 3.78

Subtract 3.78 and add 3.78 to Justin's raw score to get the 95% confidence interval

For Justin, these numbers would be:

30 – 3.78 = 26.2

30 + 3.78 = 33.8

This calculation gives you 95% confidence that Justin's true score lies somewhere between 26 and 34 (see Figure 6.1).

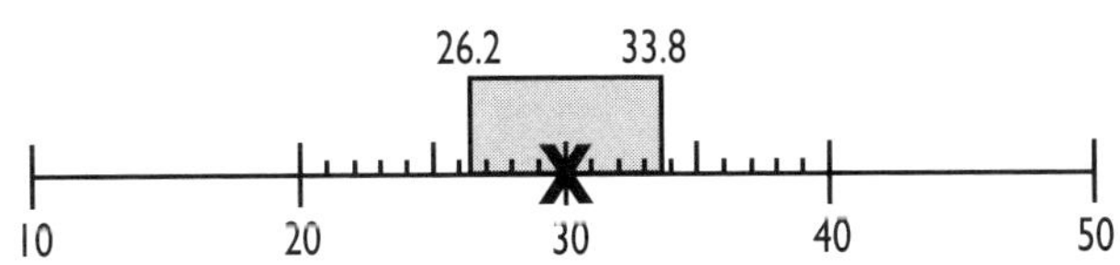

Figure 6.1 ■ Justin's Confidence Interval for Section B. Auditory Processing (10-month-old)

Sources of Validity Evidence

Terminology and the conceptualization of validity continue to be refined. Consequently, the criteria for evaluating the validity of tests and related assessment instruments continue to evolve. One of the most authoritative and current discussions of validity can be found in the *Standards for Educational and Psychological Tests* (hereafter referred to as the Test Standards) authored by a joint committee of the American Educational Research Association, the American Psychological Association and the National Council on Measurement in Education; American Research Association (AERA, 1999).

As stated in the Test Standards, "evolving conceptualizations of.... validity no longer speak of different types of validity but speak instead of lines of validity evidence, all in service of providing information relevant to a specific intended interpretation of the scores" (AERA, 1999, p. 5). First, validity is a matter of degree; it does not exist on an all-or-nothing basis. Second, validity involves an overall evaluative judgment. It requires an evaluation of the degree to which interpretations and uses of assessment results are justified by the integration of supporting evidence and is relative to the consequences of those interpretations and uses. Finally, the meaning of the term *construct* has changed and is no longer viewed as being only unobservable. The Test Standards state that the term *construct* is used "broadly as the concept or characteristic that a test is designed to measure."

The development and validation of an instrument that profiles and identifies children whose sensory processing abilities effect their functional performance and who could benefit from intervention requires that the *Infant/Toddler Sensory Profile* specifically, (1) must be shown to measure children's sensory processing abilities, (2) should correlate with other measures to the degree expected based on theory and related empirical research, and (3) should be reasonably accurate in quantifying differences between groups of children (children with various disabilities) known to have differences in sensory processing abilities being measured.

Evidence Based on Test Content

Validity evidence related to test content is supported when the content area(s) being measured are generally accepted as the proposed construct (content relevance) and when the content areas are accepted to be an adequate sampling of these areas (content coverage). Validity evidence related to the test content was established during the development of the *Infant/Toddler Sensory Profile* by conducting an exploratory study, conducting 5 review expert panels, and collecting data for a pilot study to ensure that the test sampled the full range of young children's sensory processing behaviors, that the items were placed appropriately within sections, and that they reflected Dunn's Model of Sensory Processing. (Note: these items are a summary from an article by Dunn & Daniels, under revision.)

Exploratory study. Feedback was solicited from 100 caregivers of infants and toddlers using the *Sensory Profile*, a measure of sensory processing in daily life for children 3 to 10 years of age. Caregivers were asked to respond to the items they could, cross out the items they could not answer, and write in other thoughts they had as they completed the form. Seventy-six caregivers responded; a clear developmental trend was evident in the sample. Caregivers of children ages birth to 18 months identified a majority (55–73%) of items as developmentally inappropriate for their baby. On average, parents of older children (19 to 36 months) indicated that roughly 20% of the items were inappropriate. The feedback from the caregivers resulted in some wording changes, the deletion of several items, and the creation of several new items. The new item set was used to construct the first draft of the *Infant/Toddler Sensory Profile*.

Expert Panels. Five review panels (with 5 to 7 members each) were created to review the subsequent first draft of the *Infant/Toddler Sensory Profile*. Each time, the panels were asked to sort each item by the sensory processing pattern they felt the item represented, using Dunn's Model of Sensory Processing (see Dunn, 1998). When panelists did not agree about item placement, the panelists were debriefed regarding their decision methods and perspectives on the presentation of the items. After each panel, the items were revised to improve clarity related to the conceptual model and consistency of the items for caregivers. Based on the review panels' responses, the initial version of the *Infant/Toddler Sensory Profile* was constructed. Lastly, two experts in the field were asked to review this form before finalizing the pilot version of the *Infant/Toddler Sensory Profile* (81 item version).

Pilot Study. Sixty-eight occupational therapists collected data for the factor analysis portion of the project. Researchers contacted therapists who had expressed interest in this project and those who had collected data for the *Sensory Profile* studies (see Dunn, 1999) to request their participation.

Therapists provided a sample of 401infants and toddlers (196 girls and 205 boys) ages birth to 36 months (see Dunn, 2000). Children were excluded from the study if the caregivers reported that the children were receiving early childhood services or were on regular prescription medication. The children were distributed across the United States in the following pattern: 30% from the Northeast (n = 121); 35% from the North Central (n = 140); 13% from the South (n = 53); 21% from the West (n = 85); less than 1% of families did not report region (Dunn, 2000). Eighty-five percent of the children were White, with 15% coming from other ethnic groups. The participants were distributed into rural (23%), suburban (58%), and urban (13%) groups, with just over 5% not reporting this demographic.

Several types of analyses were conducted in this study. First, descriptive statistics were compiled to identify items that may have been inappropriate for particular age groups. Multivariate Analyses of Variance (MANOVA) were done to verify the significance of age differences that appeared in the descriptive analysis.

Principal components factor analyses with varimax rotation were used to identify patterns in the data. Factor analysis for the standardization sample (see Chapter 5) provides additional evidence about the validity of the constructs embedded in the *Infant/Toddler Sensory Profile*.

Evidence Based on Relations to Other Variables

The examination of the relationship of test scores with variables external to the new test provides another source of validity evidence. Frequently, the external variables are quantified by other tests that have been established to measure the same or related constructs. When these variables are well established or accepted instruments that purport to measure the same thing, high correlations provide evidence of convergent validity. In addition, it is often important to show that the test correlates less highly with related, but different constructs. This provides evidence of discriminant validity.

Therefore, in order to provide evidence of convergent and discriminant validity for the *Infant/Toddler Sensory Profile*, we conducted a study to compare various scores obtained on the *Infant/Toddler Sensory Profile* with the *Infant/Toddler Symptom Checklist* (DeGangi, Poisson, Sickel, and Wiener; 1995).

Convergent and Discriminant Evidence

To provide evidence of convergent and discriminant validity for the *Infant/Toddler Sensory Profile*, we conducted a study to evaluate the relationship between performance on the *Infant/Toddler Sensory Profile* and selected items/sections of the *Infant/Toddler Symptom Checklist*. Eighteen caregivers provided data on both the *Infant/Toddler Sensory Profile* and the *Infant/Toddler Symptom Checklist*. Researchers hypothesized that the *Infant/Toddler Sensory Profile* is more comprehensive in the constructs tested, and therefore would have both some higher correlations (convergent validity) and some lower correlations (discriminant validity) with the *Infant/Toddler Sympton Checklist*. The actual findings from this study are provided in Table 6.3.

As stated before, convergent validity evidence is examined by investigating the relationship between scores from the test under investigation and another measure that is purported to be evaluating or measuring a similar construct.

Researchers hypothesized the following relationships, which would provide evidence of convergent validity.

- High correlations between the *Infant/Toddler Sensory Profile* and the *Infant/Toddler Symptom Checklist* for sections related to low threshold areas (i.e., Sensory Sensitivity, Sensation Avoiding, and combined Low Threshold).

Table 6.3

Correlations Between the *Infant/Toddler Sensory Profile* Quadrants and Sections and the *Infant/Toddler Symptom Checklist*

	Infant/Toddler Symptom Checklist																						
	#1	#2	#3	#4	#5	#6	#7	#8	#9	#10	#11	#12	#13	#14	#15	#16	#17	#18	#19	#20	#21	Concern	Total
Infant/Toddler Sensory Profile																							
Quadrants																							
Sensation Seeking	-.033	-.049	-.077	-.016	.091	-.049	.051	.317	-.153	.034	.111	.020	.138	.015	-.044	.166	-.034	-.078	.104	-.078	-.028	-.019	-.008
Sensory Sensitivity	.381	.250	.282	.203	.095	.117	.428	.217	.166	.580	.159	.279	.197	.204	.448	.085	.215	.384	.214	.319	.193	.338	.565
Low Registration	.142	.220	.107	.164	-.059	.088	.496	.054	-.087	.418	.338	.243	.475	.533	.387	.403	.431	.213	.264	.343	.274	.417	.624
Sensation Avoiding	.436	.181	.272	.297	.062	.149	.477	.234	.211	.486	.179	.077	.311	.276	.279	.205	.300	.300	.256	.500	.221	.478	.624
Low Threshold	.450	.208	.291	.223	.116	.148	.509	.222	.187	.513	.185	.172	.244	.218	.364	.202	.295	.371	.275	.424	.224	.441	.626
Sections																							
Auditory Processing	.111	.138	.050	.126	.074	-.031	.390	.036	-.006	.427	.284	.280	.377	.329	.432	.359	.501	.131	.244	.249	.230	.333	.511
Visual Processing	.199	.081	.085	.122	.087	-.004	.321	.355	.041	.237	.190	.320	.358	.260	.191	.255	.199	.143	.190	.192	.116	.310	.417
Tactile Processing	.165	.115	.086	.139	.098	.077	.273	.290	.106	.494	.120	.163	.197	.186	.209	.171	.091	.221	.170	.085	.227	.213	.362
Vestibular Processing	.295	.181	.182	.226	.089	.208	.402	.266	.062	.460	.221	.163	.369	.293	.289	.108	.129	.192	.143	.234	.124	.344	.486
Oral Sensory Processing	.327	.102	.260	.274	-.025	.103	.405	.345	-.091	.337	.199	-.015	.361	.274	.271	.234	.158	.246	.260	.358	.227	.341	.493
Total	.331	.152	.194	.142	.142	.094	.475	.247	.016	.479	.267	.189	.380	.311	.319	.335	.291	.289	.280	.271	.259	.386	.579

Note: Scoring for the two measures is opposite. The *Infant/Toddler Symptom Checklist* was reverse scored for the purposes of this table. High aggreement is indicated by strong positive correlations.

Table Key

>.40 >.50

Discriminant evidence of validity is provided by investigating or studying the relationship between scores from the test under investigation and another measure that is purported to be evaluating or measuring a different, or only peripherally related, construct. If such correlations are lower than the ones developed for convergent validity, such a pattern helps validate the test.

Researchers hypothesized the following relationships, which would provide evidence of discriminant validity.

- Low correlations between the *Infant/Toddler Sensory Profile* and the *Infant/Toddler Symptom Checklist* for sections related to high threshold areas (i.e., Low Registration and Sensation Seeking).

Comparison of Summary Scores

The most common associations were with level of concern and Total Score on the *Infant/Toddler Symptom Checklist*.

The total *Infant/Toddler Symptom Checklist* score correlated with 28 items on the *Infant/Toddler Sensory Profile* (with 5 of these items having correlations above .50), and the parents' ratings of their level of concern for their child correlated with 18 items on the *Infant/Toddler Sensory Profile*. Basically, when the parents reported that children engaged in *Infant/Toddler Sensory Profile* behaviors more frequently, they also expressed a higher concern about their children. When children had a higher total *Infant/Toddler Symptom Checklist* score, they also displayed more frequent *Infant/Toddler Sensory Profile* behaviors.

The total *Infant/Toddler Symptom Checklist* score had strong correlations with 9 of the 10 summary scores on the *Infant/Toddler Sensory Profile*, and had a strong correlation with the derived total *Infant/Toddler Sensory Profile* score as well. The only summary score that had a low correlation with the *Infant/Toddler Symptom Checklist* total score was Sensation Seeking, thus supporting the hypothesis that Seeking would be a distinct concept reflected in the *Infant/Toddler Sensory Profile* and not in the *Infant/Toddler Symptom Checklist*.

The parents' rating of concern for their child on the *Infant/Toddler Symptom Checklist* correlated moderately with 8 of 10 summary scores on the *Infant/Toddler Sensory Profile*.

There was also a moderate correlation with the Concern Rating and the derived total score on the *Infant/Toddler Sensory Profile*. There were no significant relationships with Visual, Tactile, and Vestibular Processing.

Comparison of Individual Items

There was also evidence of convergent and discriminant validity in individual item correlations. Here are some interesting examples along with possible explanations:

There was one individual item on the *Infant/Toddler Symptom Checklist* that had low correlations with the *Infant/Toddler Sensory Profile*: #5. "Demands adult company constantly." Perhaps this item taps a social feature of behavior that is not related to sensory processing.

There were 4 items on the *Infant/Toddler Sensory Profile* ("My child enjoys making sounds with his/her mouth," "My child finds ways to make noise with toys," "My child enjoys looking at own reflection in mirror," and "My child bumps into things, seeming not to notice objects in the way.") that had low correlations with the *Infant/Toddler Symptom Checklist*. All four of these items are Sensation Seeking items, lending additional support to the idea that Seeking is a concept unique to the *Infant/Toddler Sensory Profile*.

Some of the larger significance ratings for individual item correlations occurred between items with virtually the same focus (e.g., #10 on the *Infant/Toddler Symptom Checklist* "Distressed by having hair/face washed" and "My child becomes agitated when having hair washed" on the *Infant/Toddler Sensory Profile)*.

Summary of Evidence of Convergent and Discriminant Validity

As expected, there were large and meaningful correlations between the *Infant/Toddler Sensory Profile* and the *Infant/Toddler Symptom Checklist.* The correlations among the summary scores indicate that these relationships account for approximately 25% of the variance. As predicted, low threshold relationships were strongest.

The study findings also provide evidence of discriminant validity. Researchers found low correlations between the *Infant/Toddler Sensory Profile* and the *Infant/Toddler Symptom Checklist* for items/sections related to Sensation Seeking, suggesting that this is a unique concept reflected in the *Infant/Toddler Sensory Profile.*

Clinical Validity Evidence

Several studies were conducted with groups of children with various disabilities and a group of matched peers. See Chapter 5 for a description of the studies of children with and without disabilities.

The findings from these studies provide evidence of the measure's ability to identify those infants and toddlers with and without sensory processing difficulties that might interfere with performance in daily life.

Integrating the Evidence for Reliability and Validity for the *Infant/Toddler Sensory Profile*

This chapter provides a detailed account of the evidence base for the reliability and validity of the *Infant/Toddler Sensory Profile* scores and their use in making decisions about a child's sensory processing. Evidence about the *Infant/Toddler Sensory Profile* has been collected through the standardization process. The theoretical framework for the *Infant/Toddler Sensory Profile* and the psychometric evidence documented in this manual provides a basis for the claim that scores from the profile can provide reliable and valid inferences about a child's sensory processing abilities. The validation process, however, is not completed with the publication of the test. It is really just beginning. As stated in the Test Standards (1999), validation of a test is "a joint responsibility of the test developer and the test user. The test developer is responsible for furnishing relevant evidence and a rationale in support of the intended use of the test. The test user is ultimately responsible for evaluating the evidence in the particular setting in which the test is to be used (p. 11)." In addition to test developers and test users, independent researchers over time can also make significant contributions to the evidence base for the *Infant/Toddler Sensory Profile* by publishing relevant research on the measure in peer-reviewed journals.

CHAPTER 7

Case Studies: Interpretations and Interventions

Jessica Saiter, OTR, was my research assistant during this project, and drafted these case studies from the comments parents provided on the research versions of the *Infant/Toddler Sensory Profile*. I am grateful to her and the parents for their contributions here.

This chapter presents case studies of children who have different performance needs and contexts for performance. Although there are more features to each child's situation, the focus here is on aspects relevant to the *Infant/Toddler Sensory Profile*. These discussions provide a model for how to use the *Caregiver Questionnaire* and *Summary Score Sheet*, illustrate interpretation strategies, and suggest interventions that might be appropriate in each case.

Remember: in actual practice situations, your intervention planning will include a broader perspective about the child's performance needs and the family's needs.

Framework for Decision Making

Teams using the *Infant/Toddler Sensory Profile,* a measure of sensory responsiveness in daily life, must consider the daily life context for the child's desired performance when designing interventions. The Ecology of Human Performance (EHP) model offers a framework for constructing a broad range of interventions. This model encourages intervention designs that address the interactions among the person, the task, and the context (Dunn, Brown, & McGuigan, 1994). The five types of interventions are defined in Figure 7.1.

Although there are times when it is appropriate to design interventions that address development of better sensory processing; there also are situations that call upon the team to design a more user-friendly environment for the child so that performance can happen. People want to be able to accomplish tasks and participate with others; it would be very unpleasant to have the daily routine designed to address only weak areas of function. The EHP framework acknowledges that there are many ways to solve a performance problem, and illustrates the utility of considering task demands and

Intervention	Focus of Intervention	Definition	Example
Establish/restore	Child's strengths and needs	Interventions that improve the child's skills to perform	Have child push a cart of toys to increase proprioceptive input to the trunk and extremities to improve postural control for movements.
Adapt	Task and environmental features	Interventions that change the context or task demands to make performance more possible	Move the child's chair to minimize the number of people bumping into him so that tactile sensitivity doesn't interfere with attention and performance during mealtime.
Alter	Environmental features	Interventions that select a new context in which performance with current skills is possible	Select the day care provider whose temperament is best suited to a particular child.
Prevent	Child's strengths and needs, task and environmental features	Interventions that maintain performance by changing the course of events to keep a possible negative outcome from occurring	Design an oral-motor stimulation ritual before mealtime to prevent the child from having difficult completing the meal within the time constraints.
Create	Environmental features	Interventions that promote optimal performance by all children in that context	Collaborate in designing the optimal swimming program for all the babies.

Figure 7.1 ■ **Ecology of Human Performance: Five Types of Interventions**

environmental features in intervention (i.e., Adapt, Alter, Prevent, Create interventions). Focusing only on the person's skills and difficulties (i.e., Establish/restore interventions) limits the possibilities and is not a best practice approach (Dunn, 2001).

Many of the sensory processing difficulties identified on the *Infant/Toddler Sensory Profile* might have some effect on the child's performance. Children who have low registration will likely always be slower to respond to stimuli and have lower energy levels than other children. Their nervous systems are not designed to be overly excitable. Artful intervention honors these individual differences as part of the planning process to find the best match for each child. Part of best practice within teams and with families, includes recognizing these traits and designing interventions with individual differences in mind. You are not abandoning the child's possibility of progress by designing adaptations or changing the home to be a more suitable setting; rather you are making successful performance available to the child. Children do not have to earn the right to participate by demonstrating particular prerequisite skills; professionals have the responsibility to make participation available immediately. Data from the *Infant/Toddler Sensory Profile* can enhance the possible options for facilitating participation.

Overview

Case Study 1: Ben, a 1-month-old who is having difficulty feeding

The purpose of this case study is to illustrate how other disciplines might seek out sensory processing expertise from an occupational therapist when initial strategies are only partially effective.

Case Study 2: Trina, a 5-month-old whose parents want to make sure they are dealing with her medical and developmental status properly

The purpose of this case study is to illustrate how to interpret the *Infant/Toddler Sensory Profile* data when a child is born prematurely.

Case Study 3: Jared, a 1-year-old whose family needs help with mealtime and bedtime routines

The purpose of this case study is to illustrate how to interpret a complex pattern of scores; in this case, the combination of Low Registration and Sensory Sensitivity.

Case Study 4: Jana, an 18-month-old whose mother is concerned about limitation in diet and fussiness in different positions

The purpose of this case study is to illustrate how larger families provide a unique context for children's development, which affects their sensory processing patterns.

Case Study 5: Kaleb, a 2 1/2-year-old who is having difficulty calming self

The purpose of this case study is to illustrate how to use *Infant/Toddler Sensory Profile* results to inform professionals and parents about the meaning of defiant behaviors of a toddler with numerous sensory processing differences.

Case Study #1: Ben

Ben is a 1-month-old boy with an older sister. His mother took him to a clinic because she was having difficulties with him during feeding time. Ben has been diagnosed as having reflux. In addition to difficulties related to feeding, Ben's mother also reports that Ben seems to "fuss" more than his sister did at his age, and cries more often. The occupational therapist recommended that Ben's mother complete the *Caregiver Questionnaire* of the *Infant/Toddler Sensory Profile* (see Figure 7.2).

Scores

Ben's Sensation Seeking quadrant scores are within the Typical Performance range. Both the Sensory Sensitivity and Sensation Avoiding quadrant scores (and therefore also the Low Threshold quadrant) are within the Consult and Follow-up (More Than Others) range. Scores for the Low Registration quadrant fall in the Consult and Follow-up (Less Than Others) range. There are no Sensory Processing Section scores for infants birth to six months of age. (See Figure 7.3)

Interpretation

Ben's scores of Consult and Follow-up (More Than Others) in Sensory Sensitivity on the *Infant/Toddler Sensory Profile* reflect a pattern of overresponsiveness and indicate that Ben notices and responds to the environment more than his peers do. This is not surprising given Ben's diagnosis of reflux. As reported previously in the *User's Manual*, a study reveals that infants with reflux are significantly more likely to have increased Sensory Sensitivity (See Chapter 5, page 55). Ben's mother reported concerns about Ben's "fussiness," which can be a general expression of low thresholds.

The occupational therapist also reviewed mom's responses to specific items. It is clear that Ben displays difficulties with remaining calm or quiet in an active environment, and with getting to sleep and remaining asleep. Mom also reported that Ben was "Almost Always" irritable.

INFANT/TODDLER SENSORY PROFILE™

Winnie Dunn, Ph.D., OTR, FAOTA
with Debora B. Daniels, M.A., CCC-SLP

Caregiver Questionnaire

BIRTH TO 6 MONTHS

Child's Name: Ben Birth Date: 6-27-01 Date: 8-5-01

Completed by: Marlena Relationship to Child: mother

Service Provider's Name: Susan Discipline: OT

Was your child born prematurely? NO If so, by how many weeks? 1 week late (41 weeks)

Circle the birth order of your child within the family 1st (2nd) 3rd 4th 5th Other____

Have there been more than 3 children, between the ages of birth–18 years, living in your household during the past 12 months? NO

INSTRUCTIONS

Please check the box that **best** describes the frequency with which your child does the following behaviors. Please answer all of the statements. If you are unable to comment because you have not observed the behavior or believe that it does not apply to your child, please draw an X through the number for that item. Write any comments at the end of each section.

Use the following key to mark your responses

ALMOST ALWAYS	When presented with the opportunity, your child **almost always** responds in this manner, 90% or more of the time.
FREQUENTLY	When presented with the opportunity, your child **frequently** responds in this manner, about 75% of the time.
OCCASIONALLY	When presented with the opportunity, your child **occasionally** responds in this manner, about 50% of the time.
SELDOM	When presented with the opportunity, your child **seldom** responds in this manner, about 25% of the time.
ALMOST NEVER	When presented with the opportunity, your child **almost never** responds in this manner, 10% or less of the time.

PEARSON

1 2 3 4 5 6 7 8 9 10 11 12 A B C D E

PsychCorp

0761649573

Figure 7.2 ■ **Ben's *Caregiver Questionnaire***

Item		A. General Processing	ALMOST ALWAYS	FREQUENTLY	OCCASIONALLY	SELDOM	ALMOST NEVER
	1	My child is active throughout the day.		X_2			
—	2	My child stays quiet and calm in an active environment when compared to same age children.					X_5
—	3	My child is unaware of people coming in and going out of the room.			X_3		
	4	My child's behavior deteriorates when the schedule changes.			X_3		
	5	My child has difficulty getting to sleep and is easily awakened.	X_1				
	6	My child is irritable when compared to same age children.	X_1				

Comments

Item		B. Auditory Processing	ALMOST ALWAYS	FREQUENTLY	OCCASIONALLY	SELDOM	ALMOST NEVER
—	7	I have to speak loudly to get my child's attention.				X_4	
—	8	My child remains calm, even with sudden, everyday sounds (for example, dog barking, phone).			X_3		
—	9	I have to touch my child to gain attention.				X_4	
—	10	My child seems unaware of continuous noise in the environment (for example, TV, stereo).			X_3		
	11	My child enjoys making sounds with his/her mouth.			X_3		
—	12	My child takes a long time to respond, even to familiar voices.				X_4	
	13	My child startles easily at sound, compared to other children the same age.			X_3		
	14	My child is distracted and/or has difficulty eating in noisy environments.		X_2			
—	15	My child ignores me when I am talking.				X_4	

Comments

Figure 7.2 ■ **Ben's *Caregiver Questionnaire* (continued)**

Item		C. Visual Processing	Almost Always	Frequently	Occasionally	Seldom	Almost Never
	16	My child enjoys looking at moving or spinning objects (for example, ceiling fans, toys with wheels, floor fans).	X1				
	17	My child enjoys looking at shiny objects.				X4	
—	18	My child reacts to all faces the same way (for example, to strangers, parents, caregivers, grandparents, siblings).		X2			
	19	My child gets fussy when exposed to bright lights.			X3		
—	20	My child avoids eye contact with me.				X4	
	21	My child startles at own reflection in the mirror.					X5
|	22	My child avoids looking at toys.			X3		

Comments

Item		D. Tactile Processing	Almost Always	Frequently	Occasionally	Seldom	Almost Never
—	23	My child seems unaware of wet or dirty diapers.					X5
|	24	My child resists being held.			X3		
	25	My child becomes agitated when having hair washed.		X2			
|	26	My child avoids getting face/nose wiped.			X3		
	27	My child is distressed when having nails trimmed.		X2			
|	28	My child resists being cuddled.				X4	

Comments

Figure 7.2 ■ **Ben's *Caregiver Questionnaire (continued)***

Item		E. Vestibular Processing	Almost Always	Frequently	Occasionally	Seldom	Almost Never
—	29	My child requires more support for sitting than other children the same age (for example, infant seat, pillows, towel roll).					X 5
ᔕ	30	My child enjoys physical activity (for example, bouncing, being held up high in the air).		X 2			
—	31	My child doesn't seem to notice position changes and can be moved about with ease.				X 4	
ᔕ	32	My child enjoys rhythmical activities (for example, swinging, rocking, car rides).		X 2			
⑥	33	My child becomes upset when placed on back to change diapers.				X 4	
⑥	34	Riding in the car upsets my child.				X 4	
|	35	My child resists having head tipped back during bathing.			X 3		
⑥	36	My child cries or fusses whenever I try to move him/her.		X 2			

Comments

What do you see as your child's strengths? ______

What are your concerns? ______

STOP HERE IF YOUR CHILD IS BIRTH TO 6 MONTHS OLD..

ICON KEY	
—	Low Registration
ᔕ	Sensation Seeking
⑥	Sensory Sensitivity
|	Sensation Avoiding

SCORE KEY	
1	Almost Always
2	Frequently
3	Occasionally
4	Seldom
5	Almost Never

Figure 7.2 ■ ***Ben's Caregiver Questionnaire (continued)***

INFANT/TODDLER
SENSORY PROFILE™

Winnie Dunn, Ph.D., OTR, FAOTA

Summary Score Sheet

Child's Name: Ben — Gender: [X] Male [ ] Female

Questionnaire Completed by: Marlena

Relationship to Child: mother

Service Provider's Name: Susan

Discipline: OT

	YEAR	MONTH	DAY
Date Tested	01	~~8~~ 7	~~3~~ 35
Date of Birth	01	6	27
Chronological Age	0	1	8

The child receives the following service(s)

- [ ] Early Intervention/Preschool Services
- [X] Occupational Therapy
- [X] Other (please specify) dietician
- [ ] Physical Therapy
- [ ] Speech Therapy

Child's condition(s)

- [ ] Mental retardation
- [ ] Down Syndrome
- [ ] Speech or Language Impairment
- [ ] Autism/Pervasive Developmental Disorder (PDD)
- [ ] Developmental Delay
- [ ] Emotional disturbance or serious behavioral difficulties
- [ ] Attention disorder (ADD, ADHD)
- [ ] Visual impairment/Blindness
- [ ] Hearing impairment/Deafness
- [ ] Cerebral Palsy
- [ ] Fragile X
- [X] Reflux
- [ ] Multiple disabilities
- [ ] Traumatic brain injury
- [ ] Other neurological disorder
- [ ] Other health conditions (e.g., cardiac disorder, asthma)
- [ ] Regulatory disorder
- [ ] Other (please specify): ____

Referral concerns and other comments

Figure 7.3 ■ **Ben's *Summary Score Sheet***

Birth to 6 Months Summary Score Sheet

Quadrant Grid

Instructions: Transfer from the Caregiver Questionnaire (Birth to 6 months) the item raw score that corresponds with each item listed. Add the Raw Score column to get the Quadrant Raw Score Total for each quandrant.

QUADRANT 1 — Low Registration

Item	Raw Score
2	5
3	3
7	4
8	3
9	4
10	3
12	4
15	4
18	2
20	4
23	5
29	5
31	4
Quadrant Raw Score Total	50

QUADRANT 2 — Sensation Seeking

Item	Raw Score
1	2
11	3
16	1
17	4
30	2
32	2
Quadrant Raw Score Total	14

QUADRANT 3 — Sensory Sensitivity

Item	Raw Score
4	3
5	1
6	1
13	3
14	2
19	3
21	5
25	2
27	2
33	4
34	4
36	2
Quadrant Raw Score Total	32

QUADRANT 4 — Sensation Avoiding

Item	Raw Score
22	3
24	3
26	3
28	4
35	3
Quadrant Raw Score Total	16

ICON KEY

—	Low Registration
ʃ	Sensation Seeking
⊚	Sensory Sensitivity
|	Sensation Avoiding

Low Threshold (combined quadrant score)

Instructions: Add Sensory Sensitivity and Sensation Avoiding Quadrant Raw Score Totals to get the Low Threshold Raw Score Total

Low Threshold Raw Score Total	32 + 16 = 48

Quadrant Summary

Instructions: Transfer the Quadrant Raw Score Totals from the Birth to 6 months Quadrant Grid to the corresponding Quadrant Raw Score Total box for the appropriate ages. Plot these totals by marking an X in the appropriate classification column (Typical Performance, Consult and Follow-up)*.

Quadrant	Quadrant Raw Score Total	Less Than Others ← Consult and Follow-up	Typical Performance	→ More Than Others Consult and Follow-up
1. Low Registration (Birth–3 months)	50 /65	65 ---X--- 49	48 ---------- 39	38 ---------- 13
1. Low Registration (4–6 months)	/65	65 ---------- 52	51 ---------- 42	41 ---------- 13
2. Sensation Seeking (Birth–6 months)	14 /30	30 ---------- 16	15 -X------ 7	6
3. Sensory Sensitivity (Birth–6 months)	32 /60	60 ---------- 58	57 ---------- 45	44 --X----- 12
4. Sensation Avoiding (Birth–6 months)	16 /25	**	25 ---------- 19	18 -X------ 5
Low Threshold	**Raw Score Total**	**Note:** This score is only relevant when both Quadrants 3 and 4 are outside the Typical Performance range.		
Low Threshold (Birth–6 months)	48 /85	85 ---------- 82	81 ---------- 64	63 --X----- 17

*Classifications are based on the performance of children without disabilities ($n = 100$).
**There can be no Consult and Follow-up score for this quadrant in this age range.

Figure 7.3 ■ **Ben's *Summary Score Sheet* (continued)**

Ben displays contrasting responses with Vestibular Processing items, yet he does show difficulty with position changes, fussing and noticing when he is moved. Ben does, however, enjoy rhythmical activities and physical activity.

As the occupational therapist reviewed both quadrant scores and individual item responses with Ben's mother, they discussed activities that could facilitate an optimal sensory environment and minimize sensitivity behaviors during daily routines. Ben's mother reported that in addition to physical and rhythmical activities, he enjoys looking at moving or spinning objects. This presented an opportunity for the therapist to point out the sensory processing characteristics of these activities.

Mom commented that because many items on the *Caregiver Questionnaire* asked about activities that did not seem related to eating, she didn't understand their connection to Ben's "fussiness." She anticipated that Ben's difficulty was only related to his medical problems. Mom believed that Ben's reflux made him cry and be irritable, much the way she herself felt when she had heartburn. She felt the formula recommended by the dietician might be more helpful than occupational therapy. She didn't see how sights and noises could have very much effect on Ben's ability to eat.

Intervention

Ben's mother decided initially to see the effects of using the special formula. Ben spit up less, but feedings still lasted longer than normal due to Ben's "fussiness." The mother recalled her conversation with the occupational therapist about how sights and sounds may affect Ben. The dietician and parent discussed this issue and decided it might be helpful to contact the occupational therapist for additional information.

During the following visits, the therapist and mother explored the effect of different mealtime arrangements. The family routine was to feed Ben in the TV room while his preschool-age sister was watching and singing along with cartoons. Ben's mother felt more in control of both children when they were close, and said she often worried about being neglectful of Ben's sister because it takes a long time to feed Ben. The therapist suggested that the variable volume and intensity of noises and sights from the TV and from Ben's sister could add up to create a type of sensory overload for Ben's overresponsive sensory system. The mother suggested that the kitchen might be quieter, but she still felt badly about Ben's sister. The therapist discussed ways to give Ben's sister some responsibility during feeding (e.g., getting the blanket ready, helping to hold the bottle, stroking Ben's head or arm). Mom was delighted with the idea that Ben's sister could be part of this time, and was eager to explore possibilities. She had wanted to include the sister, but had worried that Ben's irritability would cause the interaction to be "bad" for Ben or his sister or both. Ben's sister was also eager to join the activity, and did not seem to miss the cartoon time at all.

The therapist also noted that the ceiling fan in the kitchen might be calming because Ben's mother reported an "Almost Always" response for Item 16: "My child enjoys looking at moving or spinning objects (for example, ceiling fans,...)."

As the therapist and parent continued exploring the impact of sensory processing on typical, everyday activities, the therapist demonstrated techniques to provide firm support and security to Ben during position changes and discussed ways to plan ahead to minimize unnecessary handling. The therapist explained that placement in more upright positions, especially during and after mealtimes, may improve physiologic functioning and reduce irritability associated with effects of reflux. It was noted that Ben likes physical activity, especially gentle rhythmical bouncing; the therapist showed mom some strategies to incorporate this, yet told mom to use caution about using them just after mealtime. For example, they discussed the fact that Ben enjoys being held upright at his mother's shoulder while she walks around the house.

Outcomes on Intervention

After a few months, Ben's mother reported that she was able to feed him in an acceptable amount of time, and that including Ben's sister had created a wonderful time for the three of them to bond. Because Ben drinks from a bottle, his father has been able to join in the feeding activities, with pointers from Ben's sister. Mom set up the kitchen so that Ben can relax on an elevated wedge and concentrate on drinking from his bottle. She also reported that using the ceiling fan in his bedroom helps him go to sleep at night. The mother and therapist decided to stop regular visits and resume contact if any future concerns arose.

Case Study #2: Trina

Trina is a 5-month-old girl who was born nine weeks prematurely. Trina spent her first 5 weeks in a neonatal intensive care unit in a nearby city. Since her family lives in a rural area, this was a stressful time for them, although with six immediate family members they all got into a routine for visiting and keeping Trina company. She has four older siblings, two of whom are living with her parents. Although she is now at home, her family continues to deal with her medical and developmental concerns. The occupational therapist on the High Risk Follow-up Team suggested the *Infant/Toddler Sensory Profile* as part of the follow-up assessment (see Figure 7.4).

Scores

Trina has scores in the Typical Performance range in the Low Registration, Sensory Seeking, and Sensory Sensitivity quadrants. Her scores are within the Consult and Follow-up (More Than Others) range in the Sensation Avoiding quadrant, an expected response when taking her prematurity into consideration (See Figure 7.5).

Interpretation

The therapist completed the *Summary Score Sheet* from the information on the *Caregiver Questionnaire*. Since most of Trina's scores are in the Typical Performance range, these findings provided encouraging evidence of areas of development in which Trina is performing like other children her age.

The therapist wanted to reassure the family of Trina's positive developmental indicators, because families often have worries with a baby who was born prematurely. As noted in Chapter 5 (p. 41), Trina's pattern of scores are consistent with a trend in which premature babies have more frequent low threshold responses (Sensation Avoiding and/or Sensory Sensitivity). Although premature infants tend to be hyperresponsive during early development, data from the *User's Manual* show that these effects of prematurity fade as the child has increased opportunities to experience sensations. Because Trina is 5 months old and her Sensation Avoiding score is just one point below the Typical Performance cut score, the therapist hypothesizes that this mild sensitivity will be resolved in the next few months.

The parents began to discuss their concerns about Trina being medically fragile due to her prematurity and their fears about doing something harmful to her. The therapist acknowledged their concerns, and assured them that this is a common issue for families who have a child that has a fragile beginning. Families of premature infants may have a tendency to limit sensory experiences in order to protect the child from additional stress. The therapist and family discussed safe ways to play with Trina, and this built up everyone's confidence.

INFANT/TODDLER SENSORY PROFILE™

Winnie Dunn, Ph.D., OTR, FAOTA
with Debora B. Daniels, M.A., CCC-SLP

Caregiver Questionnaire

BIRTH TO 6 MONTHS

Child's Name: Trina Birth Date: 12-8-00 Date: 5-13-01

Completed by: Aaron Relationship to Child: Father

Service Provider's Name: Susan Discipline: OT

Was your child born prematurely? Yes If so, by how many weeks? 9 weeks (31 weeks gestation)

Circle the birth order of your child within the family 1st 2nd 3rd 4th (5th) Other_____

Have there been more than 3 children, between the ages of birth–18 years, living in your household during the past 12 months? No

INSTRUCTIONS

Please check the box that **best** describes the frequency with which your child does the following behaviors. Please answer all of the statements. If you are unable to comment because you have not observed the behavior or believe that it does not apply to your child, please draw an X through the number for that item. Write any comments at the end of each section.

Use the following key to mark your responses

ALMOST ALWAYS	When presented with the opportunity, your child **almost always** responds in this manner, 90% or more of the time.
FREQUENTLY	When presented with the opportunity, your child **frequently** responds in this manner, about 75% of the time.
OCCASIONALLY	When presented with the opportunity, your child **occasionally** responds in this manner, about 50% of the time.
SELDOM	When presented with the opportunity, your child **seldom** responds in this manner, about 25% of the time.
ALMOST NEVER	When presented with the opportunity, your child **almost never** responds in this manner, 10% or less of the time.

PEARSON

Printed in the United States of America.
1 2 3 4 5 6 7 8 9 10 11 12 A B C D E

PsychCorp

0761649573

Figure 7.4 ■ Trina's *Caregiver Questionnaire*

Item		A. General Processing	ALMOST ALWAYS	FREQUENTLY	OCCASIONALLY	SELDOM	ALMOST NEVER
	1	My child is active throughout the day.		X 2			
—	2	My child stays quiet and calm in an active environment when compared to same age children.	X 1				
—	3	My child is unaware of people coming in and going out of the room.					X 5
	4	My child's behavior deteriorates when the schedule changes.					X 5
	5	My child has difficulty getting to sleep and is easily awakened.					X 5
	6	My child is irritable when compared to same age children.					X 5

Comments

Item		B. Auditory Processing	ALMOST ALWAYS	FREQUENTLY	OCCASIONALLY	SELDOM	ALMOST NEVER
—	7	I have to speak loudly to get my child's attention.					X 5
—	8	My child remains calm, even with sudden, everyday sounds (for example, dog barking, phone).	X 1				
—	9	I have to touch my child to gain attention.					X 5
—	10	My child seems unaware of continuous noise in the environment (for example, TV, stereo).					X 5
	11	My child enjoys making sounds with his/her mouth.		X 2			
—	12	My child takes a long time to respond, even to familiar voices.					X 5
	13	My child startles easily at sound, compared to other children the same age.				X 4	
	14	My child is distracted and/or has difficulty eating in noisy environments.					X 5
—	15	My child ignores me when I am talking.				X 4	

Comments

Figure 7.4 ■ **Trina's *Caregiver Questionnaire* (continued)**

Item		C. Visual Processing	Almost Always	Frequently	Occasionally	Seldom	Almost Never
	16	My child enjoys looking at moving or spinning objects (for example, ceiling fans, toys with wheels, floor fans).		X2			
	17	My child enjoys looking at shiny objects.			X3		
—	18	My child reacts to all faces the same way (for example, to strangers, parents, caregivers, grandparents, siblings).		X2			
	19	My child gets fussy when exposed to bright lights.			X3		
—	20	My child avoids eye contact with me.					X5
	21	My child startles at own reflection in the mirror.					X5
|	22	My child avoids looking at toys.				X4	

Comments

Item		D. Tactile Processing	Almost Always	Frequently	Occasionally	Seldom	Almost Never
—	23	My child seems unaware of wet or dirty diapers.					X5
|	24	My child resists being held.					X5
	25	My child becomes agitated when having hair washed.					X5
|	26	My child avoids getting face/nose wiped.		X2			
	27	My child is distressed when having nails trimmed.					X5
|	28	My child resists being cuddled.					X5

Comments

Figure 7.4 ■ **Trina's *Caregiver Questionnaire* (continued)**

Item		E. Vestibular Processing	Almost Always	Frequently	Occasionally	Seldom	Almost Never
—	29	My child requires more support for sitting than other children the same age (for example, infant seat, pillows, towel roll).				X 4	
∫	30	My child enjoys physical activity (for example, bouncing, being held up high in the air).	X 1				
—	31	My child doesn't seem to notice position changes and can be moved about with ease.	X 1				
∫	32	My child enjoys rhythmical activities (for example, swinging, rocking, car rides).	X 1				
@	33	My child becomes upset when placed on back to change diapers.					X 5
@	34	Riding in the car upsets my child.					X 5
|	35	My child resists having head tipped back during bathing.		X 2			
@	36	My child cries or fusses whenever I try to move him/her.					X 5

Comments

What do you see as your child's strengths? ______

What are your concerns? ______

STOP HERE IF YOUR CHILD IS BIRTH TO 6 MONTHS OLD..

ICON KEY	
—	Low Registration
∫	Sensation Seeking
@	Sensory Sensitivity
|	Sensation Avoiding

SCORE KEY	
1	Almost Always
2	Frequently
3	Occasionally
4	Seldom
5	Almost Never

Figure 7.4 ■ ***Trina's Caregiver Questionnaire (continued)***

INFANT/TODDLER
SENSORY PROFILE™

Winnie Dunn, Ph.D., OTR, FAOTA

Summary Score Sheet

Child's Name: Trina

Gender: ☐ Male ☒ Female

Questionnaire Completed by: Aaron

Relationship to Child: Father

Service Provider's Name: Susan

Discipline: OT

	YEAR	MONTH	DAY
Date Tested	~~01~~ 00	~~5~~ 17	13
Date of Birth	00	12	8
Chronological Age	0	5	5

The child receives the following service(s)

- ☐ Early Intervention/Preschool Services
- ☐ Occupational Therapy
- ☒ Other (please specify) Medical care
- ☐ Physical Therapy
- ☐ Speech Therapy

Child's condition(s)

- ☐ Mental retardation
- ☐ Down Syndrome
- ☐ Speech or Language Impairment
- ☐ Autism/Pervasive Developmental Disorder (PDD)
- ☐ Developmental Delay
- ☐ Emotional disturbance or serious behavioral difficulties
- ☐ Attention disorder (ADD, ADHD)
- ☐ Visual impairment/Blindness
- ☐ Hearing impairment/Deafness
- ☐ Cerebral Palsy
- ☐ Fragile X
- ☐ Reflux
- ☐ Multiple disabilities
- ☐ Traumatic brain injury
- ☐ Other neurological disorder
- ☐ Other health conditions (e.g., cardiac disorder, asthma)
- ☐ Regulatory disorder
- ☒ Other (please specify): premature

Referral concerns and other comments

Figure 7.5 ■ **Trina's *Summary Score Sheet***

Birth to 6 Months Summary Score Sheet

Quadrant Grid

Instructions: Transfer from the Caregiver Questionnaire (Birth to 6 months) the item raw score that corresponds with each item listed. Add the Raw Score column to get the Quadrant Raw Score Total for each quadrant.

— QUADRANT 1	
Low Registration	
Item	Raw Score
2	1
3	5
7	5
8	1
9	5
10	5
12	5
15	4
18	2
20	5
23	5
29	4
31	1
Quadrant Raw Score Total	48

QUADRANT 2	
Sensation Seeking	
Item	Raw Score
1	2
11	2
16	2
17	3
30	1
32	1
Quadrant Raw Score Total	11

QUADRANT 3	
Sensory Sensitivity	
Item	Raw Score
4	5
5	5
6	5
13	4
14	5
19	3
21	5
25	5
27	5
33	5
34	5
36	5
Quadrant Raw Score Total	57

QUADRANT 4	
Sensation Avoiding	
Item	Raw Score
22	4
24	5
26	2
28	5
35	2
Quadrant Raw Score Total	18

ICON KEY
— Low Registration
Sensation Seeking
Sensory Sensitivity
Sensation Avoiding

Low Threshold (combined quadrant score)

Instructions: Add Sensory Sensitivity and Sensation Avoiding Quadrant Raw Score Totals to get the Low Threshold Raw Score Total

Low Threshold Raw Score Total	57 + 18 = 75

Quadrant Summary

Instructions: Transfer the Quadrant Raw Score Totals from the Birth to 6 months Quadrant Grid to the corresponding Quadrant Raw Score Total box for the appropriate ages. Plot these totals by marking an X in the appropriate classification column (Typical Performance, Consult and Follow-up)*.

Quadrant	Quadrant Raw Score Total	Less Than Others ← Consult and Follow-up	Typical Performance	→ More Than Others Consult and Follow-up
1. Low Registration (Birth–3 months)	/65	66 — 49	48 ---------- 39	38 ---------- 13
1. Low Registration (4–6 months)	48 /65	65 ---------- 52	51 --X----- 42	41 ---------- 13
2. Sensation Seeking (Birth–6 months)	11 /30	30 ---------- 16	15 --X---- 7	6
3. Sensory Sensitivity (Birth–6 months)	57 /60	60 ---------- 58	X ---------- 45	44 ---------- 12
4. Sensation Avoiding (Birth–6 months)	18 /25	**	25 ---------- 19	X ---------- 5
Low Threshold	**Raw Score Total**	**Note:** This score is only relevant when both Quadrants 3 and 4 are outside the Typical Performance range.		
Low Threshold (Birth–6 months)	/85	85 ---------- 82	81 ---------- 64	63 ---------- 17

*Classifications are based on the performance of children without disabilities ($n = 100$).
**There can be no Consult and Follow-up score for this quadrant in this age range.

Figure 7.5 ■ **Trina's *Summary Score Sheet* (continued)**

Intervention

At the next team meeting, the occupational therapist communicated Trina's Typical Performance scores from the *Infant/Toddler Sensory Profile*, including the prediction about Trina's Sensation Avoiding resolving itself in the next few months. She also described her suggestions for providing ongoing appropriate developmental experiences to support Trina's development in a safe and graded manner. The therapist also discussed how to make activities harder or easier as Trina's development progesses and as her health status fluctuates over time. The parents decided they wanted to consult with the therapist over the telephone and by email in the future, since Trina was in such an active developmental state. They also wanted to have a family meeting with their other children and the therapist and discuss the therapy strategies so that everyone could feel comfortable interacting with Trina. The parents wanted all their children to feel close to Trina, and they recognized from their experiences parenting the others that having contact is the best way to ensure that close family feeling.

Outcomes on Intervention

Since Trina was their fifth child, her parents were more aware of typical child development than other parents might have been. They voiced their concern at Trina being "behind" her brothers and sisters at this age. Her parents appreciated information about Trina's strengths, as they had been focusing on concerns for the past few months.

At the next follow-up visit (about six months later), the therapist observed Trina in her home. She noted that, as they had discussed by email, all the family members engaged with Trina and that a variety of appropriate toys were available to her. During conversations with the family, they discussed Trina's gains, the resolution of her Sensation Avoiding concerns, and the family's demonstration of interactions and developmental support. Trina's participation in the follow-up program continued although OT services were no longer felt necessary. The family was reassured that these services could be considered again if additional developmental concerns occurred.

Case Study #3: Jared

Jared is a 1-year-old boy whose family participated in the community's Child Find Program. The Child Find team confirmed the diagnosis of developmental delay due to Jared's developmental milestone scores on the screening measures. His pediatrician had already detected some delays and solicited help for the family from a community physical therapist. Jared currently receives physical therapy at home and daycare. The physical therapist referred Jared and his parents to an occupational therapist when Jared's parents asked about his difficulty at meals and bedtime. During a discussion of family routines at a recent neighborhood gathering, the parents realized that Jared's routines did not match those of other children who were his age. The occupational therapist sent an *Infant/Toddler Sensory Profile* along with a cover letter to his family prior to their first visit. See Figure 7.6 for a completed *Caregiver Questionnaire* for Jared.

Scores

Jared's quadrant scores are within the Definite Difference (More Than Others) range in the Low Registration quadrant and the Probable Difference (More Than Others) range in the Sensory Sensitivity quadrant. Scores fall in the Typical Performance range for Sensation Seeking and Sensation Avoiding (See Figure 7.7). Section scores fall in the Definite Difference (More Than Others) range for Auditory Processing and the Probable Difference (More Than Others) range for Visual Processing. Tactile, Vestibular, and Oral Sensory Processing are within the Typical Performance range.

INFANT/TODDLER SENSORY PROFILE™

Winnie Dunn, Ph.D., OTR, FAOTA
with Debora B. Daniels, M.A., CCC-SLP

Caregiver Questionnaire

7 TO 36 MONTHS

Child's Name: Jared Birth Date: 4-19-00 Date: 5-2-01

Completed by: Julie Relationship to Child: mother

Service Provider's Name: Becca Discipline: OT

Circle the birth order of your child within the family 1st (2nd) 3rd 4th 5th Other____

Have there been more than 3 children, between the ages of birth–18 years, living in your household during the past 12 months? No

INSTRUCTIONS

Please check the box that **best** describes the frequency with which your child does the following behaviors. Please answer all of the statements. If you are unable to comment because you have not observed the behavior or believe that it does not apply to your child, please draw an X through the number for that item. Write any comments at the end of each section.

Use the following key to mark your responses

ALMOST ALWAYS	When presented with the opportunity, your child **almost always** responds in this manner, 90% or more of the time.
FREQUENTLY	When presented with the opportunity, your child **frequently** responds in this manner, about 75% of the time.
OCCASIONALLY	When presented with the opportunity, your child **occasionally** responds in this manner, about 50% of the time.
SELDOM	When presented with the opportunity, your child **seldom** responds in this manner, about 25% of the time.
ALMOST NEVER	When presented with the opportunity, your child **almost never** responds in this manner, 10% or less of the time.

ISBN 076164957-3

PEARSON

1 2 3 4 5 6 7 8 9 10 11 12 A B C D E

PsychCorp

9 780761 649571

Figure 7.6 ■ **Jared's *Caregiver Questionnaire***

Item		A. General Processing	ALMOST ALWAYS	FREQUENTLY	OCCASIONALLY	SELDOM	ALMOST NEVER
	1	My child's behavior deteriorates when the schedule changes.		X_2			
|	2	My child avoids playing with others.					X_5
|	3	My child withdraws from situations.					X_5

Note: You do not calculate a Raw Score Total for this section.

Comments

Item		B. Auditory Processing	ALMOST ALWAYS	FREQUENTLY	OCCASIONALLY	SELDOM	ALMOST NEVER
—	4	I have to speak loudly to get my child's attention.			X_3		
—	5	I have to touch my child to gain attention.			X_3		
	6	My child enjoys making sounds with his/her mouth.	X_1				
—	7	My child takes a long time to respond, even to familiar voices.					X_5
	8	My child startles easily at sound, compared to other children the same age.			X_3		
	9	My child is distracted and/or has difficulty eating in noisy environments.	X_1				
—	10	My child ignores me when I am talking.					X_5
|	11	My child tries to escape from noisy environments.			X_3		
	12	My child finds ways to make noise with toys.	X_1				
—	13	It takes a long time for my child to respond to his/her name when it is called.			X_3		
		Section Raw Score Total	28				

Comments #8: If you are out of the room and come in and greet him, he will "jump" like you scared him
#9: He's more interested in TV or what's going on at a restaurant than eating

Item		C. Visual Processing	ALMOST ALWAYS	FREQUENTLY	OCCASIONALLY	SELDOM	ALMOST NEVER
	14	My child enjoys looking at moving or spinning objects (for example, ceiling fans, toys with wheels, floor fans).	X_1				
	15	My child enjoys looking at shiny objects.		X_2			
—	16	My child avoids eye contact with me.					X_5
|	17	My child refuses to look at books with me.					X_5
—	18	My child does not recognize self in the mirror.	X_1				
	19	My child enjoys looking at own reflection in the mirror.	X_1				
	20	My child prefers fast-paced, brightly colored TV shows.	X_1				
		Section Raw Score Total	16				

Comments

Figure 7.6 ■ **Jared's *Caregiver Questionnaire* (continued)**

Item		D. Tactile Processing	Almost Always	Frequently	Occasionally	Seldom	Almost Never
|	21	My child resists being held.		X_2			
◎	22	My child becomes agitated when having hair washed.					X_5
|	23	My child avoids getting face/nose wiped.				X_4	
◎	24	My child is distressed when having nails trimmed.		X_2			
|	25	My child resists being cuddled.		X_2			
◎	26	My child is upset by changes in the bath water temperature, from one bath to the next.					X_5
|	27	My child avoids contact with rough or cold surfaces (for example, squirms, arches, cries).					X_5
◎	28	My child becomes very upset if own clothing, hands, and/or face are messy.		X_2			
◎	29	My child gets upset with extreme differences in room temperature (for example, hotter, colder).					X_5
◎	30	My child becomes anxious when walking or crawling on certain surfaces (for example, grass, sand, carpet, tile).				X_4	
ʃ	31	My child enjoys playing with food.			X_3		
ʃ	32	My child seeks opportunities to feel vibrations (for example, stereo speakers, washer, dryer).					X_5
—	33	My child bumps into things, seeming to not notice objects in the way.			X_3		
ʃ	34	My child enjoys splashing during bath time.	X_1				
ʃ	35	My child uses hands to explore food and other textures.				X_4	
		Section Raw Score Total	52				

Comments

Item		E. Vestibular Processing	Almost Always	Frequently	Occasionally	Seldom	Almost Never
—	36	My child requires more support for sitting than other children the same age (for example, infant seat, pillows, towel roll).			X_3		
ʃ	37	My child enjoys physical activity (for example, bouncing, being held up high in the air).	X_1				
ʃ	38	My child enjoys rhythmical activities (for example, swinging, rocking, car rides).			X_3		
◎	39	My child becomes upset when placed on back to change diapers.					X_5
|	40	My child resists having head tipped back during bathing.					X_5
◎	41	My child cries or fusses whenever I try to move him/her.					X_5
		Section Raw Score Total	22				

Comments #38: Doesn't like car rides, won't sleep during trips and doesn't like mom/dad to rock him but will rock his head back and forth to sleep.

Figure 7.6 ■ **Jared's *Caregiver Questionnaire* (continued)**

Item		F. Oral Sensory Processing	Almost Always	Frequently	Occasionally	Seldom	Almost Never
Sensation Seeking	42	My child licks/chews on nonfood objects.	X 1				
Sensation Seeking	43	My child mouths objects.	X 1				
—	44	My child is unaware of food or liquid left on lips.					X 5
|	45	My child refuses all but a few food choices.			X 3		
|	46	My child resists having teeth brushed.					X 5
—	47	My child refuses to drink from a cup.					X 5
|	48	My child refuses to try new foods.					X 5
		Section Raw Score Total	25				

Comments

What do you see as your child's strengths? Enjoys "checking things out"

What are your concerns? The slightest noise awakens him from sleep (nap, bedtimes, etc.)

STOP HERE IF YOUR CHILD IS 7 TO 36 MONTHS OLD.

ICON KEY	
—	Low Registration
Sensation Seeking icon	Sensation Seeking
Sensory Sensitivity icon	Sensory Sensitivity
|	Sensation Avoiding

SCORE KEY	
1	Almost Always
2	Frequently
3	Occasionally
4	Seldom
5	Almost Never

Figure 7.6 ■ **Jared's *Caregiver Questionnaire* (continued)**

INFANT/TODDLER

SENSORY PROFILE™

Winnie Dunn, Ph.D., OTR, FAOTA

Summary Score Sheet

Child's Name: Jared

Gender: ☒ Male ☐ Female

Questionnaire Completed by: Julie

Relationship to Child: mother

Service Provider's Name: Becca

Discipline: OT

	YEAR	MONTH	DAY
Date Tested	01	~~5~~ 4	~~2~~ 32
Date of Birth	00	4	19
Chronological Age	1	0	13

The child receives the following service(s)

- ☐ Early Intervention/Preschool Services
- ☒ Occupational Therapy
- ☒ Other (please specify) Attends daycare
- ☒ Physical Therapy
- ☐ Speech Therapy

Child's condition(s)

- ☐ Mental retardation
- ☐ Down Syndrome
- ☐ Speech or Language Impairment
- ☐ Autism/Pervasive Developmental Disorder (PDD)
- ☒ Developmental Delay
- ☐ Emotional disturbance or serious behavioral difficulties
- ☐ Attention disorder (ADD, ADHD)
- ☐ Visual impairment/Blindness
- ☐ Hearing impairment/Deafness
- ☐ Cerebral Palsy
- ☐ Fragile X
- ☐ Reflux
- ☐ Multiple disabilities
- ☐ Traumatic brain injury
- ☐ Other neurological disorder
- ☐ Other health conditions (e.g., cardiac disorder, asthma)
- ☐ Regulatory disorder
- ☐ Other (please specify): ______

Referral concerns and other comments

#8: If you are out of the room and come in and greet him, he will "jump" like you scared him

#9: He's more interested in TV or what's going on at a restaurant than eating

#33: Doesn't like car rides, won't sleep during trips and doesn't like mom/dad to rock him but will rock his head back and forth to sleep.

Figure 7.7 ■ **Jared's *Summary Score Sheet***

7 to 36 Months Summary Score Sheet

Quadrant Grid

Instructions: Transfer from the Caregiver Questionnaire (7 to 36 months) the item raw score that corresponds with each item listed. Add the Raw Score column to get the Quadrant Raw Score Total for each quadrant.

QUADRANT 1 — Low Registration

Item	Raw Score
4	3
5	3
7	5
10	5
13	3
16	5
18	1
33	3
36	3
44	5
47	5
Quadrant Raw Score Total	41

QUADRANT 2 — Sensation Seeking

Item	Raw Score
6	1
12	1
14	1
15	2
19	1
20	1
31	3
32	5
34	1
35	4
37	1
38	3
42	1
43	1
Quadrant Raw Score Total	26

QUADRANT 3 — Sensory Sensitivity

Item	Raw Score
1	2
8	3
9	1
22	5
24	2
26	5
28	2
29	5
30	4
39	5
41	5
Quadrant Raw Score Total	39

QUADRANT 4 — Sensation Avoiding

Item	Raw Score
2	5
3	5
11	3
17	5
21	2
23	4
25	2
27	5
40	5
45	3
46	5
48	5
Quadrant Raw Score Total	49

ICON KEY

- — Low Registration
- ʃ Sensation Seeking
- ๑ Sensory Sensitivity
- | Sensation Avoiding

Low Threshold (combined quadrant score)

Instructions: Add Sensory Sensitivity and Sensation Avoiding Quadrant Raw Score Totals to get the Low Threshold Raw Score Total

Low Threshold Raw Score Total: 39 + 49 = 88

Quadrant Summary

Instructions: Transfer the Quadrant Raw Score Totals from the 7 to 36 months Quadrant Grid to the corresponding Quadrant Raw Score Total box for the appropriate ages. Plot these totals by marking an X in the appropriate classification column (Typical Performance, Probable Difference, Definite Difference)*.

Quadrant	Quadrant Raw Score Total	Less Than Others ← Definite Difference	Less Than Others ← Probable Difference	Typical Performance	→ More Than Others Probable Difference	→ More Than Others Definite Difference
1. Low Registration (7–36 months)	41 /55	**	55	54 ---------- 46	45 ---------- 43	42 -X------- 11
2. Sensation Seeking (7–12 months)	26 /70	70 ---------- 44	43 ---------- 36	35 ---X---- 19	18 ---------- 14	**
2. Sensation Seeking (13–18 months)	/70	70 ---------- 46	45 ---------- 38	37---------- 20	19 ---------- 14	**
2. Sensation Seeking (19–24 months)	/70	70 ---------- 50	49 ---------- 42	41 ---------- 25	24 ---------- 16	15 ---------- 14
2. Sensation Seeking (25–30 months)	/70	70 ---------- 50	49 ---------- 43	42 ---------- 27	26 ---------- 19	18 ---------- 14
2. Sensation Seeking (31–36 months)	/70	70 ---------- 59	58 ---------- 49	48 ---------- 28	27 ---------- 18	17 ---------- 14
3. Sensory Sensitivity (7–36 months)	39 /55	**	55 ---------- 53	52 ---------- 41	40 X------- 36	35 ---------- 11
4. Sensation Avoiding (7–36 months)	49 /60	**	60 ---------- 57	56 ----X-- 45	44 ---------- 39	38 ---------- 12
Low Threshold	**Raw Score Total**	**Note:** This score is only relevant when both Quadrants 3 and 4 are outside the Typical Performance range.				
Low Threshold (7–36 months)	/115	**	115 ---------- 108	107 ---------- 87	86 ---------- 77	76 ---------- 23

*Classifications are based on the performance of children without disabilities ($n = 489$).
**There can be no Definite Difference for this section in this age range.

Figure 7.7 ■ **Jared's *Summary Score Sheet* (continued)**

Sensory Processing Section Summary (7 to 36 Months)

Instructions: Transfer the Section Raw Score Totals from the 7 to 36 months Caregiver Questionnaire to the corresponding Section Raw Score Total box for the appropriate ages. Plot these totals by marking an X in the appropriate classification column (Typical Performance, Probable Difference, Definite Difference)*.

Sensory Processing Section	Section Raw Score Total	Less Than Others ←		Typical Performance	→ More Than Others	
		Definite Difference	Probable Difference		Probable Difference	Definite Difference
A. General Processing	No section raw score total is calculated for the General Processing Section.					
B. Auditory Processing (7–36 months)	28 /50	50 ------ 48	47 ------ 44	43 ------ 35	34 ------ 31	30 X ------ 10
C. Visual Processing (7–36 months)	16 /35	35 ------ 32	31 ------ 28	27 ------ 20	19 ------ 16 X	15 ------ 7
D. Tactile Processing (7–24 months)	52 /75	75 ------ 68	67 ------ 62	61 ---X--- 48	47 ------ 42	41 ------ 15
D. Tactile Processing (25–36 months)	/75	75 ------ 72	71 ------ 65	64 ------ 51	50 ------ 44	43 ------ 15
E. Vestibular Processing (7–36 months)	22 /30	30 ------ 27	26 ------ 24	23 X ------ 18	17 ------ 15	14 ------ 6
F. Oral Sensory Processing (7–12 months)	25 /35	35 ------ 33	32 ------ 30	29 ---X--- 21	20 ------ 17	16 ------ 7
F. Oral Sensory Processing (13–18 months)	/35	**	35 ------ 32	31 ------ 23	22 ------ 19	18 ------ 7
F. Oral Sensory Processing (19–24 months)	/35	**	35 ------ 33	32 ------ 24	23 ------ 20	19 ------ 7
F. Oral Sensory Processing (25–30 months)	/35	**	35 ------ 33	32 ------ 25	24 ------ 22	21 ------ 7
F. Oral Sensory Processing (31–36 months)	/35	**	35 ------ 34	33 ------ 25	24 ------ 21	20 ------ 7

*Classifications are based on the performance of children without disabilities ($n = 489$)
**There can be no Definite Difference for this section in this age range.

Note: Reproducible Growth Curves for Children 7 to 36 months, for Sensation Seeking, Tactile Processing, and Oral Sensory Processing, are available in Appendix A of the *Infant/Toddler Sensory Profile User's Manual.*

ISBN 076164959-X

PEARSON

Printed in the United States of America.
1 2 3 4 5 6 7 8 9 10 11 12 A B C D E

PsychCorp

Visit www.SensoryProfile.com for additional information and updates.

9 780761 649595

Figure 7.7 ■ **Jared's *Summary Score Sheet* (continued)**

Interpretation

Generally, the scores provided some support and explanation for why Jared might be having the difficulties the family outlined in their referral concerns. For example, the family is concerned about Jared's bedtime routine and his easy awakening during the night. The *Infant/Toddler Sensory Profile* scores indicated some difficulty with low threshold stimuli (Sensory Sensitivity), which might indicate distractions have a greater possibility of keeping Jared from settling down. These sensitivities seem to be in the area of Auditory and, to a lesser extent, Visual Processing.

The quadrant scores indicate a Definite Difference in Low Registration and a Probable Difference in Sensory Sensitivity. This is an interesting combination, since one score seemingly reflects missing stimuli or a lack of noticing (Low Registration), and the other score reflects frequent noticing (Sensory Sensitivity). Children with low registration are hypothesized to have inadequate neural activation to support performance and therefore may miss salient cues in the context to support ongoing activity. Interventions should focus on enhancing task features and contextual cues in the activities of interest by increasing the contrast of stimuli or decreasing predictability (increasing novelty and arousal input).

In contrast, children with Sensory Sensitivity tend to be distractible. They do not need any more arousal or alerting stimuli; they need discriminatory input that supports organized patterns of information to the brain without generating additional arousal. Discriminatory input includes firm touch-pressure on the surface of the skin (rather than light touch), linear patterns of movement (rather than angular movement such as spinning or bending over), and predictable patterns of visual and auditory cues (rather than unexpected stimuli).

The presence of Low Thresholds and Low Registration indicates poor modulation. Children with this combination may not notice stimuli when they need to but once they do notice, their nervous systems are intolerant to input. Their extremely small processing range for sensory information creates a difficult situation for parents and therapists. An effective intervention incorporates elements of increased contrast but must have structure to highlight the salient cues without overloading a sensitive system.

The occupational therapist considered examples from Jared's life to use when explaining this. She reflected that it was hard for family members to get Jared's attention (e.g., when calling his name), yet the TV or stereo distracted him and his parents report that the slightest noise wakes him up at night and disrupts his sleep cycle.

Although the parents were already aware of Jared's difficulties, the occupational therapist was able to organize all the observations and test scores into a cohesive picture that informed the family about the meaning of Jared's behaviors. With these insights, the parents could understand Jared better, and participate more actively in generating intervention ideas.

Intervention

After reviewing the information from the *Infant/Toddler Sensory Profile* together, the therapist and family decided to focus on mealtime first. Jared tends to notice the television or other people rather than focus on eating. His mother moved his high chair to face toward a wall instead of into the TV room. This helped to decrease visual and auditory distractions. Mom preferred to keep the television on because it kept his sister's attention while she focused on Jared's mealtime routines.

Once the family understood the underlying reasons for Jared's behaviors, they were able to apply the same concepts when eating out. As a family, they began to select booths since the high walls tended to cut down on visual distractions and ambient noise from the restaurant. With Jared showing less distractibility, the family members were able to interact with each other more during these outings.

In addition, the therapist suggested adding high contrast visual cues to focus Jared's attention towards his food during the meal without overstimulating him with random stimuli. His mother purchased a plastic placemat with contrasting surfaces on the top and bottom. She began to routinely place the mat so it contrasted with Jared's plate and food, and he would be drawn to looking at his own plate. His parents also wondered if Jared was distracted at mealtime when he saw that they had different foods than he did. Because he was just now being introduced to "grown-up" food, the family decided to emphasize the transition to table foods as an avenue to hold Jared's attention. His parents began to provide chopped-up and mashed portions of their food to assist Jared in eating in an acceptable amount of time.

As the family's comfort at the dinner table grew, the team looked at his sleeping patterns. Jared utilized a very specific ritual to prepare himself for bedtime. He preferred a very quiet, dark room after his bottle. He then rocked his head back and forth while slamming his leg on the mattress. If redirected by being held or rocked, he would not go to sleep. His family relayed that this was the <u>only</u> successful routine for Jared to fall asleep. They said that in conversations with friends who have children Jared's age, they have become aware that Jared's ritual was unusual. However, they felt it achieved the goal of falling asleep, and so had mixed feelings about whether or not to intervene. The other team members supported the family in their acceptance of Jared's ritual. The occupational therapist also pointed out that this story revealed Jared's adaptive skills. Jared was effective in finding ways to obtain calming input (e.g., head rocking, leg banging, darkness, quiet).

The therapist suggested that the family could also help Jared sleep by taking opportunities to reduce noises from the rest of the house. The therapist described the difference between alerting sounds (e.g., unexpected footsteps, laughter from the television) and calming sounds (e.g., a familiar song or continuous "white" noise, such as a ceiling fan). With this information, the family decided to try playing lullabies in Jared's room at night. The goal was to offer consistent auditory input, decreasing his opportunities to notice unexpected noises.

Outcomes on Intervention

After changing the position of the highchair in the kitchen, his mother reported that Jared was less distracted during meal times. He finished his meals in a time frame acceptable to his family. His parents also noticed that decreasing distractions during meals enabled them to eat out more often. When they offered him the same food as the rest of the family, he focused his attention on eating rather than on comparing his food with others' plates. The placemat seemed to make Jared feel special, and increased his interest in his own plate. His parents reported being very pleased with these improvements.

As focus changed to Jared's sleeping patterns, they evaluated different approaches. First, his mother and father played an album of lullabies after placing him in his crib. That helped for the first hour, but after the music stopped, outside noises continued to wake him up. Next, they lowered the volume of the TV and put a box fan in his room, since the fan wouldn't "run out" during the night as the music had been doing.

This decreased the likelihood of disrupting Jared's sleep, since the white noise provided constant calming input throughout the night. The family decided to continue using this method, since Jared woke up less often.

Case Study #4: Jana

Jana is an 18-month-old girl with four adolescent aunts and uncles in the household. She and her mother live at her grandmother's, who cares for her between daycare and her mother coming home from classes at the university. At grandmother's insistence, the mother brought Jana to the early intervention program at the neighborhood school. Both were concerned about Jana's limited diet and crying when in certain positions, particularly lying on her stomach. Jana received a diagnosis of a developmental delay during the team's assessment process. An occupational therapist and physical therapist are members of her early intervention team. Her mother reported concerns about Jana's limited diet and crying when in certain positions, particularly lying on her stomach. The occupational therapist considered the possible contribution of sensory processing to Jana's difficulties, and recommended that her mother complete the *Caregiver Questionnaire* of the *Infant/Toddler Sensory Profile* (see Figure 7.8).

Scores

Jana is like other children her age on most areas of sensory processing. Her Sensory Seeking score indicates she seeks stimuli less than other children.

Interpretation

The occupational therapist completed the *Summary Score Sheet* of the *Infant/Toddler Sensory Profile*. She noted that Jana's scores indicated that she processes sensory information much like other children her age. Probable Difference in Sensory Seeking indicates that she seeks LESS sensory information than other children her age.

The occupational therapist hypothesized that since Jana didn't seek out and explore the environment around her, she had a negative reaction when presented with alerting sensory information, like being positioned on her stomach. Therefore, she planned to gather information about situations in which Jana does seek out sensory input. By considering both high and low seeking situations, the therapist thought she might be able to identify patterns that would inform them about intervention options.

In addition, the occupational therapist remembered from the manual that children who live in families with more than four siblings have lower seeking scores. The author hypothesized that with larger families, younger children do not have to generate their own sensory stimuli as actively. The therapist had noted during previous visits that Jana's teenage aunts and uncles created a rich sensory environment during their daily routines (e.g., playing fast-tempo music, watching television, occasionally roughhousing). The therapist decided to bring these ideas up at the meeting, with the suggestion that Jana's seeking is probably fine for a child in her circumstance.

These hypotheses did not change the fact that the family expressed concern about daily life activities, and that the occupational therapist would need to address these issues with the family.

INFANT/TODDLER SENSORY PROFILE™

Winnie Dunn, Ph.D., OTR, FAOTA
with Debora B. Daniels, M.A., CCC-SLP

Caregiver Questionnaire

7 TO 36 MONTHS

Child's Name: Jana Birth Date: 1-8-00 Date: 6-27-01

Completed by: Maria Relationship to Child: mother

Service Provider's Name: Heather Discipline: OT

Circle the birth order of your child within the family (1st) 2nd 3rd 4th 5th Other______

Have there been more than 3 children, between the ages of birth–18 years, living in your household during the past 12 months? Yes

INSTRUCTIONS

Please check the box that **best** describes the frequency with which your child does the following behaviors. Please answer all of the statements. If you are unable to comment because you have not observed the behavior or believe that it does not apply to your child, please draw an X through the number for that item. Write any comments at the end of each section.

Use the following key to mark your responses

ALMOST ALWAYS	When presented with the opportunity, your child **almost always** responds in this manner, 90% or more of the time.
FREQUENTLY	When presented with the opportunity, your child **frequently** responds in this manner, about 75% of the time.
OCCASIONALLY	When presented with the opportunity, your child **occasionally** responds in this manner, about 50% of the time.
SELDOM	When presented with the opportunity, your child **seldom** responds in this manner, about 25% of the time.
ALMOST NEVER	When presented with the opportunity, your child **almost never** responds in this manner, 10% or less of the time.

ISBN 076164957-3

PEARSON

Printed in the United States of America.
1 2 3 4 5 6 7 8 9 10 11 12 A B C D E

PsychCorp

9 780761 649571

Figure 7.8 ■ Jana's *Caregiver Questionnaire*

Item	A. General Processing	ALMOST ALWAYS	FREQUENTLY	OCCASIONALLY	SELDOM	ALMOST NEVER
1	My child's behavior deteriorates when the schedule changes.	X1				
2	My child avoids playing with others.					X5
3	My child withdraws from situations.			X3		

Note: You do not calculate a Raw Score Total for this section.

Comments

#1: Jana gets very upset when her schedule changes.

Item	B. Auditory Processing	ALMOST ALWAYS	FREQUENTLY	OCCASIONALLY	SELDOM	ALMOST NEVER
4	I have to speak loudly to get my child's attention.					X5
5	I have to touch my child to gain attention.					X5
6	My child enjoys making sounds with his/her mouth.	X1				
7	My child takes a long time to respond, even to familiar voices.					X5
8	My child startles easily at sound, compared to other children the same age.				X4	
9	My child is distracted and/or has difficulty eating in noisy environments.				X4	
10	My child ignores me when I am talking.					X5
11	My child tries to escape from noisy environments.					X5
12	My child finds ways to make noise with toys.		X2			
13	It takes a long time for my child to respond to his/her name when it is called.					X5
	Section Raw Score Total	41				

Comments

Item	C. Visual Processing	ALMOST ALWAYS	FREQUENTLY	OCCASIONALLY	SELDOM	ALMOST NEVER
14	My child enjoys looking at moving or spinning objects (for example, ceiling fans, toys with wheels, floor fans).			X3		
15	My child enjoys looking at shiny objects.			X3		
16	My child avoids eye contact with me.					X5
17	My child refuses to look at books with me.					X5
18	My child does not recognize self in the mirror.					X5
19	My child enjoys looking at own reflection in the mirror.	X1				
20	My child prefers fast-paced, brightly colored TV shows.			X3		
	Section Raw Score Total	25				

Comments

Figure 7.8 ■ **Jana's *Caregiver Questionnaire* (continued)**

Item		D. Tactile Processing	Almost Always	Frequently	Occasionally	Seldom	Almost Never
I	21	My child resists being held.					X5
◎	22	My child becomes agitated when having hair washed.				X4	
I	23	My child avoids getting face/nose wiped.			X3		
◎	24	My child is distressed when having nails trimmed.				X4	
I	25	My child resists being cuddled.					X5
◎	26	My child is upset by changes in the bath water temperature, from one bath to the next.			X3		
I	27	My child avoids contact with rough or cold surfaces (for example, squirms, arches, cries).			X3		
◎	28	My child becomes very upset if own clothing, hands, and/or face are messy.				X4	
◎	29	My child gets upset with extreme differences in room temperature (for example, hotter, colder).				X4	
◎	30	My child becomes anxious when walking or crawling on certain surfaces (for example, grass, sand, carpet, tile).					X5
ʃ	31	My child enjoys playing with food.				X4	
ʃ	32	My child seeks opportunities to feel vibrations (for example, stereo speakers, washer, dryer).				X4	
—	33	My child bumps into things, seeming to not notice objects in the way.					X5
ʃ	34	My child enjoys splashing during bath time.	X1				
ʃ	35	My child uses hands to explore food and other textures.			X3		
		Section Raw Score Total	57				

Comments

Item		E. Vestibular Processing	Almost Always	Frequently	Occasionally	Seldom	Almost Never
—	36	My child requires more support for sitting than other children the same age (for example, infant seat, pillows, towel roll).					X5
ʃ	37	My child enjoys physical activity (for example, bouncing, being held up high in the air).					X5
ʃ	38	My child enjoys rhythmical activities (for example, swinging, rocking, car rides).	X1				
◎	39	My child becomes upset when placed on back to change diapers.				X4	
I	40	My child resists having head tipped back during bathing.	X1				
◎	41	My child cries or fusses whenever I try to move him/her.				X4	
		Section Raw Score Total	20				

Comments

#37: Jana does not like being held above your head, she gets very scared. Also, she cries when you place her on her tummy.

Figure 7.8 ■ **Jana's *Caregiver Questionnaire* (continued)**

Item		F. Oral Sensory Processing	Almost Always	Frequently	Occasionally	Seldom	Almost Never
ʃ	42	My child licks/chews on nonfood objects.				X 4	
ʃ	43	My child mouths objects.					X 5
—	44	My child is unaware of food or liquid left on lips.					X 5
|	45	My child refuses all but a few food choices.				X 4	
|	46	My child resists having teeth brushed.					X 5
—	47	My child refuses to drink from a cup.				X 4	
|	48	My child refuses to try new foods.			X 3		
		Section Raw Score Total	30				

Comments

#48: Jana won't eat slimy foods like Jello, pudding, etc.

What do you see as your child's strengths? ____________

What are your concerns? ____________

STOP HERE IF YOUR CHILD IS 7 TO 36 MONTHS OLD.

ICON KEY	
—	Low Registration
ʃ	Sensation Seeking
◎	Sensory Sensitivity
|	Sensation Avoiding

SCORE KEY	
1	Almost Always
2	Frequently
3	Occasionally
4	Seldom
5	Almost Never

Figure 7.8 ■ **Jana's *Caregiver Questionnaire (continued)***

INFANT/TODDLER
SENSORY PROFILE™

Winnie Dunn, Ph.D., OTR, FAOTA

Summary Score Sheet

Child's Name: Jana Gender: ☐ Male ☒ Female

Questionnaire Completed by: Maria

Relationship to Child: mother

Service Provider's Name: Heather

Discipline: OT

	YEAR	MONTH	DAY
Date Tested	01	6	27
Date of Birth	00	1	8
Chronological Age	1	5	19

The child receives the following service(s)

- ☒ Early Intervention/Preschool Services
- ☒ Occupational Therapy
- ☐ Other (please specify) ______
- ☒ Physical Therapy
- ☐ Speech Therapy

Child's condition(s)

- ☐ Mental retardation
- ☐ Down Syndrome
- ☐ Speech or Language Impairment
- ☐ Autism/Pervasive Developmental Disorder (PDD)
- ☒ Developmental Delay
- ☐ Emotional disturbance or serious behavioral difficulties
- ☐ Attention disorder (ADD, ADHD)
- ☐ Visual impairment/Blindness
- ☐ Hearing impairment/Deafness
- ☐ Cerebral Palsy
- ☐ Fragile X
- ☐ Reflux
- ☐ Multiple disabilities
- ☐ Traumatic brain injury
- ☐ Other neurological disorder
- ☐ Other health conditions (e.g., cardiac disorder, asthma)
- ☐ Regulatory disorder
- ☐ Other (please specify): ______

Referral concerns and other comments

#1: Jana gets very upset when her schedule changes.
#37: Jana does not like being held above your head, she gets very scared. Also, she cries when you place her on her tummy.
#48: Jana won't eat slimy foods like Jello, pudding, etc.

Figure 7.9 ■ **Jana's *Summary Score Sheet***

7 to 36 Months Summary Score Sheet

Quadrant Grid

Instructions: Transfer from the Caregiver Questionnaire (7 to 36 months) the item raw score that corresponds with each item listed. Add the Raw Score column to get the Quadrant Raw Score Total for each quadrant.

QUADRANT 1 — Low Registration

Item	Raw Score
4	5
5	5
7	5
10	5
13	5
16	5
18	5
33	5
36	5
44	5
47	5
Quadrant Raw Score Total	55

QUADRANT 2 — Sensation Seeking

Item	Raw Score
6	1
12	2
14	3
15	3
19	1
20	3
31	4
32	4
34	1
35	3
37	5
38	1
42	3
43	4
Quadrant Raw Score Total	38

QUADRANT 3 — Sensory Sensitivity

Item	Raw Score
1	1
8	4
9	4
22	4
24	4
26	3
28	4
29	4
30	5
39	4
41	4
Quadrant Raw Score Total	41

QUADRANT 4 — Sensation Avoiding

Item	Raw Score
2	5
3	3
11	5
17	5
21	5
23	3
25	5
27	3
40	1
45	4
46	5
48	4
Quadrant Raw Score Total	48

ICON KEY
Low Registration
Sensation Seeking
Sensory Sensitivity
Sensation Avoiding

Low Threshold (combined quadrant score)

Instructions: Add Sensory Sensitivity and Sensation Avoiding Quadrant Raw Score Totals to get the Low Threshold Raw Score Total

Low Threshold Raw Score Total	41 + 48 = 89

Quadrant Summary

Instructions: Transfer the Quadrant Raw Score Totals from the 7 to 36 months Quadrant Grid to the corresponding Quadrant Raw Score Total box for the appropriate ages. Plot these totals by marking an X in the appropriate classification column (Typical Performance, Probable Difference, Definite Difference)*.

		Less Than Others ←			→ More Than Others	
Quadrant	**Quadrant Raw Score Total**	**Definite Difference**	**Probable Difference**	**Typical Performance**	**Probable Difference**	**Definite Difference**
1. Low Registration (7–36 months)	55 /55	**	X	54 ---------- 46	45 ---------- 43	42 ---------- 11
2. Sensation Seeking (7–12 months)	/70	70 ---------- 44	43 ---------- 36	35 ---------- 19	18 ---------- 14	**
2. Sensation Seeking (13–18 months)	38 /70	70 ---------- 46	45 ---------- 38 X	37 ---------- 20	19 ---------- 14	**
2. Sensation Seeking (19–24 months)	/70	70 ---------- 50	49 ---------- 42	41 ---------- 25	24 ---------- 16	15 ---------- 14
2. Sensation Seeking (25–30 months)	/70	70 ---------- 50	49 ---------- 43	42 ---------- 27	26 ---------- 19	18 ---------- 14
2. Sensation Seeking (31–36 months)	/70	70 ---------- 59	58 ---------- 49	48 ---------- 28	27 ---------- 18	17 ---------- 14
3. Sensory Sensitivity (7–36 months)	41 /55	**	55 ---------- 53	52 ---------- X	40 ---------- 36	35 ---------- 11
4. Sensation Avoiding (7–36 months)	48 /60	**	60 ---------- 57	56 ---------- X 45	44 ---------- 39	38 ---------- 12
Low Threshold	**Raw Score Total**	**Note:** This score is only relevant when both Quadrants 3 and 4 are outside the Typical Performance range.				
Low Threshold (7–36 months)	/115	**	115 ---------- 108	107 ---------- 87	86 ---------- 77	76 ---------- 23

*Classifications are based on the performance of children without disabilities ($n = 489$).
**There can be no Definite Difference for this section in this age range.

Figure 7.9 ■ **Jana's *Summary Score Sheet* (continued)**

Sensory Processing Section Summary (7 to 36 Months)

Instructions: Transfer the Section Raw Score Totals from the 7 to 36 months Caregiver Questionnaire to the corresponding Section Raw Score Total box for the appropriate ages. Plot these totals by marking an X in the appropriate classification column (Typical Performance, Probable Difference, Definite Difference)*.

		Less Than Others ←			→ More Than Others	
Sensory Processing Section	**Section Raw Score Total**	**Definite Difference**	**Probable Difference**	**Typical Performance**	**Probable Difference**	**Definite Difference**
A. General Processing	No section raw score total is calculated for the General Processing Section.					
B. Auditory Processing (7–36 months)	41 /50	50 ------- 48	47 ---------- 44	43 --X------ 35	34 ---------- 31	30 ---------- 10
C. Visual Processing (7–36 months)	25 /35	35-------- 32	31 ---------- 28	27 --X------ 20	19 ---------- 16	15 ---------- 7
D. Tactile Processing (7–24 months)	57 /75	75 ------- 68	67 ---------- 62	61 --X------ 48	47 ---------- 42	41 ---------- 15
D. Tactile Processing (25–36 months)	/75	75-------- 72	71 ---------- 65	64 ---------- 51	50 ---------- 44	43 ---------- 15
E. Vestibular Processing (7–36 months)	20 /30	30-------- 27	26 ---------- 24	23 ---X--- 18	17 ---------- 15	14 ---------- 6
F. Oral Sensory Processing (7–12 months)	/35	35-------- 33	32 ---------- 30	29 ---------- 21	20 ---------- 17	16 ---------- 7
F. Oral Sensory Processing (13–18 months)	30 /35	**	35 ---------- 32	31 X-------- 23	22 ---------- 19	18 ---------- 7
F. Oral Sensory Processing (19–24 months)	/35	**	35 ---------- 33	32 ---------- 24	23 ---------- 20	19 ---------- 7
F. Oral Sensory Processing (25–30 months)	/35	**	35 ---------- 33	32 ---------- 25	24 ---------- 22	21 ---------- 7
F. Oral Sensory Processing (31–36 months)	/35	**	35 ---------- 34	33 ---------- 25	24 ---------- 21	20 ---------- 7

*Classifications are based on the performance of children without disabilities ($n = 489$)
**There can be no Definite Difference for this section in this age range.

Note: Reproducible Growth Curves for Children 7 to 36 months, for Sensation Seeking, Tactile Processing, and Oral Sensory Processing, are available in Appendix A of the *Infant/Toddler Sensory Profile User's Manual.*

ISBN 076164959-X
9 780761 649595

PEARSON

Printed in the United States of America.
1 2 3 4 5 6 7 8 9 10 11 12 A B C D E

PsychCorp

Visit www.SensoryProfile.com for additional information and updates.

Figure 7.9 ■ **Jana's *Summary Score Sheet (continued)***

Intervention

The team decided the occupational therapist should focus on interventions for mealtime and the physical therapist would address Jana's movement concerns. The physical therapist reported that Jana's motor skills were behind her peers. The occupational therapist hypothesized that Jana's low number of seeking vestibular activities heightened the family's concern over her low interest in movement. The occupational therapist shared her hypotheses about Jana's lower need for engaging with the environment due to the high activity level in the home, which provided Jana with lots of stimulation that she did not have to generate for herself. One of the aunts commented about the family's willingness to carry Jana around and accommodate her. "We sort of treat her like our baby doll" was this aunt's comment. She even said that there was competition sometimes to play with Jana, and that perhaps they could all push her a little to engage in movement.

Another aunt reported that Jana didn't get upset when the boys roughhoused with her; "even when they pass her like a football, she doesn't react very much." Therefore, the therapists asked the aunt to videotape a roughhousing session so they could watch together and gain a greater insight into Jana's responses. The aunts and uncles found this videotaping suggestion appealing, and turned it into an invitation to create an "epic film of Jana's life." The team consulted mainly by telephone, email, and through a series of videotapes across several months.

As for mealtime, the therapist noted Jana did explore food with her hands. Therefore, she suggested using food exploration to increase Jana's diet. Since she does not prefer soft foods (e.g., applesauce, mashed potatoes, pudding) from a spoon, they tried introducing them as finger foods. For example, her mother offered Jana animal crackers (a preferred food) to dip into the pudding. Next, she showed her daughter how to lick off any excess pudding from her hands. Grandmother offered to take tastes with her own fingers on her own plate as a way to model eating softer foods. One of the aunts asked if they could finger paint with pudding, but grandmother was afraid this would unleash a food fight among the older children, and asked that they not implement that idea.

Outcomes on Intervention

The physical therapist reported that Jana started to explore activities that provide a high amount of vestibular information as the uncles restrained themselves from being so active during roughhousing. They began to see that as they invited Jana more, and provided less of the movement themselves, she picked up her own movements to get them to react. They began videotaping Jana regularly to add to the "documentary" of her life, and actually provided great data for the therapists of Jana's progress.

One of the aunts began to use rhythmical movements and songs while playing with her. For example, they would play "Horsey" by sitting Jana on a knee and bouncing to the rhythm of a song.

An uncle noted that Jana would briefly get down on her stomach when searching for a preferred toy under the coffee table. Therefore, the family decided to move some of Jana's toys to a container that encouraged this movement. By placing an ottoman in front of the toy box, Jana was encouraged to climb up and lie down to reach for a toy. The occupational therapist was delighted to see her exploration on the documentary film the aunts and uncles provided each quarter. During their follow-up conference call, she explained that Jana's movement and interest (i.e., seeking) behaviors were all improved.

After a few months, Jana's diet included the thicker, soft foods (pudding, mashed potatoes). Her mother reported that using a preferred food along with the soft food created the most success. She continued to experiment with this technique (e.g., adding pears to Jell-O®). For a birthday celebration, grandmother relented and they all fingerpainted with icing, pudding, and cake sprinkles for added interest.

Case Study #5: Kaleb

Kaleb is a 2½-year-old boy who is an only child. Since he was 6 months old, Kaleb was often irritable and had difficulty with self-calming. He always cried while being held and when riding in the car. He also withdrew from situations when upset by "shutting down." He would stop interacting with both his parents and his usual favorite toys. His family visited a developmental team for help, and consulted with a developmental pediatrician, an occupational therapist, and a developmental psychologist. They gave Kaleb a diagnosis of Regulatory Disorder (Zero to Three, 1994). While his self-calming abilities have improved and his irritability has diminished, he continues to have a very limited diet and resists his parents during self-care activities (e.g., bathing and brushing teeth). The occupational therapist on the team had been consulting periodically with the family; during infancy the family had completed the Birth to 6 months version of the *Infant/Toddler Sensory Profile*, so she asked them to complete the 7 to 36 months version (see Figure 7.10).

Scores

Kaleb's Sensation Seeking and Low Registration quadrant scores are within the Typical Performance range. Both the Sensory Sensitivity and Sensation Avoiding quadrant scores (and therefore also the Low Threshold quadrant) are within the Definite Difference (More Than Others) range. Kaleb's section scores fall in the Definite Difference range for Tactile and Vestibular Processing, the Probable Difference range for Auditory and Oral Sensory Processing, and the Typical Performance range for Visual Processing (See Figure 7.11).

Interpretation

Kaleb's extreme scores in the low threshold quadrants (Sensory Sensitivity and Sensation Avoiding) provide evidence of continued challenges with sensory input. Children who have Sensory Sensitivity tend to be distractible and may display hyperactivity. It has been hypothesized that children who have Sensory Sensitivity have overreactive neural systems that make them aware of every stimulus that becomes available, and these children do not have the commensurate ability to habituate to these stimuli. Children with Sensory Sensitivity do not need additional alerting or arousal stimuli; they need stimuli of a discriminatory nature such as firm touch, linear patterns of movement, and predictable patterns of visual and auditory cues.

Children who have Sensation Avoiding behaviors tend to work to actively keep their thresholds from being met. It has been hypothesized that meeting thresholds is uncomfortable or frightening to the child. These children may try to keep these events at bay by either withdrawing, engaging in emotional outbursts, or creating rituals (which limits unfamiliar stimuli). Children who avoid sensation have a narrow range of stimuli that are acceptable. They are resistant to change because change represents an opportunity to be bombarded with unfamiliar stimuli. Forcing a child to "get used to" and to confront intense sensory input without systematic planning generates more defiant and withdrawing behaviors. Intervention requires that teams construct events to introduce a wider range of sensory experiences gradually and respectfully so the child can develop habituation for them. The overall goal is to honor the child's need to limit unfamiliar sensory input and gradually broaden the sensory experiences within the child's accepted rituals.

INFANT/TODDLER SENSORY PROFILE™

Winnie Dunn, Ph.D., OTR, FAOTA
with Debora B. Daniels, M.A., CCC-SLP

Caregiver Questionnaire

7 TO 36 MONTHS

Child's Name: Kaleb Birth Date: 2-8-99 Date: 8-21-01

Completed by: Eva and Aidan Relationship to Child: parents

Service Provider's Name: Lily Discipline: OT

Circle the birth order of your child within the family (1st) 2nd 3rd 4th 5th Other______

Have there been more than 3 children, between the ages of birth–18 years, living in your household during the past 12 months? No

INSTRUCTIONS

Please check the box that **best** describes the frequency with which your child does the following behaviors. Please answer all of the statements. If you are unable to comment because you have not observed the behavior or believe that it does not apply to your child, please draw an X through the number for that item. Write any comments at the end of each section.

Use the following key to mark your responses

ALMOST ALWAYS	When presented with the opportunity, your child **almost always** responds in this manner, 90% or more of the time.
FREQUENTLY	When presented with the opportunity, your child **frequently** responds in this manner, about 75% of the time.
OCCASIONALLY	When presented with the opportunity, your child **occasionally** responds in this manner, about 50% of the time.
SELDOM	When presented with the opportunity, your child **seldom** responds in this manner, about 25% of the time.
ALMOST NEVER	When presented with the opportunity, your child **almost never** responds in this manner, 10% or less of the time.

ISBN 076164957-3

PEARSON

Printed in the United States of America.
1 2 3 4 5 6 7 8 9 10 11 12 A B C D E

PsychCorp

9 780761 649571

Figure 7.10 ■ **Kaleb's *Caregiver Questionnaire***

Item		A. General Processing	ALMOST ALWAYS	FREQUENTLY	OCCASIONALLY	SELDOM	ALMOST NEVER
@	1	My child's behavior deteriorates when the schedule changes.			X3		
❘	2	My child avoids playing with others.			X3		
❘	3	My child withdraws from situations.			X3		

Note: You do not calculate a Raw Score Total for this section.

Comments

#3: Used to be "Almost Always" but he's improved so much

Item		B. Auditory Processing	ALMOST ALWAYS	FREQUENTLY	OCCASIONALLY	SELDOM	ALMOST NEVER
—	4	I have to speak loudly to get my child's attention.			X3		
—	5	I have to touch my child to gain attention.				X4	
ʃ	6	My child enjoys making sounds with his/her mouth.		X2			
—	7	My child takes a long time to respond, even to familiar voices.				X4	
@	8	My child startles easily at sound, compared to other children the same age.	X1				
@	9	My child is distracted and/or has difficulty eating in noisy environments.		X2			
—	10	My child ignores me when I am talking.				X4	
❘	11	My child tries to escape from noisy environments.				X4	
ʃ	12	My child finds ways to make noise with toys.		X2			
—	13	It takes a long time for my child to respond to his/her name when it is called.					X5
		Section Raw Score Total	31				

Comments

Item		C. Visual Processing	ALMOST ALWAYS	FREQUENTLY	OCCASIONALLY	SELDOM	ALMOST NEVER
ʃ	14	My child enjoys looking at moving or spinning objects (for example, ceiling fans, toys with wheels, floor fans).	X1				
ʃ	15	My child enjoys looking at shiny objects.			X3		
—	16	My child avoids eye contact with me.			X3		
❘	17	My child refuses to look at books with me.					X5
—	18	My child does not recognize self in the mirror.					X5
ʃ	19	My child enjoys looking at own reflection in the mirror.			X3		
ʃ	20	My child prefers fast-paced, brightly colored TV shows.	X1				
		Section Raw Score Total	21				

Comments

Figure 7.10 ■ **Kaleb's *Caregiver Questionnaire* (continued)**

Item	D. Tactile Processing	Almost Always	Frequently	Occasionally	Seldom	Almost Never
21	My child resists being held.			X_3		
22	My child becomes agitated when having hair washed.			X_3		
23	My child avoids getting face/nose wiped.			X_3		
24	My child is distressed when having nails trimmed.	X_1				
25	My child resists being cuddled.		X_2			
26	My child is upset by changes in the bath water temperature, from one bath to the next.	X_1				
27	My child avoids contact with rough or cold surfaces (for example, squirms, arches, cries).			X_3		
28	My child becomes very upset if own clothing, hands, and/or face are messy.		X_2			
29	My child gets upset with extreme differences in room temperature (for example, hotter, colder).			X_3		
30	My child becomes anxious when walking or crawling on certain surfaces (for example, grass, sand, carpet, tile).			X_3		
31	My child enjoys playing with food.		X_2			
32	My child seeks opportunities to feel vibrations (for example, stereo speakers, washer, dryer).				X_4	
33	My child bumps into things, seeming to not notice objects in the way.					X_5
34	My child enjoys splashing during bath time.		X_2			
35	My child uses hands to explore food and other textures.				X_4	
	Section Raw Score Total	41				

Comments

#21: Used to be "Almost Always" but he's slowly improved

Item	E. Vestibular Processing	Almost Always	Frequently	Occasionally	Seldom	Almost Never
36	My child requires more support for sitting than other children the same age (for example, infant seat, pillows, towel roll).					X_5
37	My child enjoys physical activity (for example, bouncing, being held up high in the air).	X_1				
38	My child enjoys rhythmical activities (for example, swinging, rocking, car rides).			X_3		
39	My child becomes upset when placed on back to change diapers.	X_1				
40	My child resists having head tipped back during bathing.	X_1				
41	My child cries or fusses whenever I try to move him/her.			X_3		
	Section Raw Score Total	14				

Comments

Figure 7.10 ■ **Kaleb's *Caregiver Questionnaire* (continued)**

Item		F. Oral Sensory Processing	Almost Always	Frequently	Occasionally	Seldom	Almost Never
ʃ	42	My child licks/chews on nonfood objects.					X 5
ʃ	43	My child mouths objects.					X 5
—	44	My child is unaware of food or liquid left on lips.			X 3		
|	45	My child refuses all but a few food choices.	X 1				
|	46	My child resists having teeth brushed.		X 2			
—	47	My child refuses to drink from a cup.					X 5
|	48	My child refuses to try new foods.	X 1				
		Section Raw Score Total	22				

Comments

What do you see as your child's strengths? ____________________

What are your concerns? ____________________

STOP HERE IF YOUR CHILD IS 7 TO 36 MONTHS OLD.

ICON KEY	
—	Low Registration
ʃ	Sensation Seeking
◎	Sensory Sensitivity
|	Sensation Avoiding

SCORE KEY	
1	Almost Always
2	Frequently
3	Occasionally
4	Seldom
5	Almost Never

Figure 7.10 ■ **Kaleb's *Caregiver Questionnaire* (continued)**

INFANT/TODDLER
SENSORY PROFILE™

Winnie Dunn, Ph.D., OTR, FAOTA

Summary Score Sheet

Child's Name: Kaleb   Gender: ☒ Male ☐ Female

Questionnaire Completed by: Eva and Aidan

Relationship to Child: parents

Service Provider's Name: Lily

Discipline: OT

	YEAR	MONTH	DAY
Date Tested	01	8	21
Date of Birth	99	2	8
Chronological Age	2	6	13

The child receives the following service(s)

- ☐ Early Intervention/Preschool Services
- ☒ Occupational Therapy
- ☒ Other (please specify) developmental psychologist and pediatrician
- ☐ Physical Therapy
- ☐ Speech Therapy

Child's condition(s)

- ☐ Mental retardation
- ☐ Down Syndrome
- ☐ Speech or Language Impairment
- ☐ Autism/Pervasive Developmental Disorder (PDD)
- ☐ Developmental Delay
- ☐ Emotional disturbance or serious behavioral difficulties
- ☐ Attention disorder (ADD, ADHD)
- ☐ Visual impairment/Blindness
- ☐ Hearing impairment/Deafness
- ☐ Cerebral Palsy
- ☐ Fragile X
- ☐ Reflux
- ☐ Multiple disabilities
- ☐ Traumatic brain injury
- ☐ Other neurological disorder
- ☐ Other health conditions (e.g., cardiac disorder, asthma)
- ☒ Regulatory disorder
- ☐ Other (please specify): ______

Referral concerns and other comments

#3: Used to be "Almost Always" but he's improved so much (withdraws from situations)

#21: Used to be "Almost Always" but he's slowly improved (resists being held)

Figure 7.11 ■ **Kaleb's *Summary Score Sheet***

7 to 36 Months Summary Score Sheet

Quadrant Grid

Instructions: Transfer from the Caregiver Questionnaire (7 to 36 months) the item raw score that corresponds with each item listed. Add the Raw Score column to get the Quadrant Raw Score Total for each quadrant.

QUADRANT 1 — Low Registration

Item	Raw Score
4	3
5	4
7	4
10	4
13	5
16	3
18	5
33	5
36	5
44	3
47	5
Quadrant Raw Score Total	46

QUADRANT 2 — Sensation Seeking

Item	Raw Score
6	2
12	2
14	1
15	3
19	3
20	1
31	2
32	4
34	2
35	4
37	1
38	3
42	5
43	5
Quadrant Raw Score Total	38

QUADRANT 3 — Sensory Sensitivity

Item	Raw Score
1	3
8	1
9	2
22	3
24	1
26	1
28	2
29	3
30	3
39	1
41	3
Quadrant Raw Score Total	23

QUADRANT 4 — Sensation Avoiding

Item	Raw Score
2	3
3	3
11	4
17	5
21	3
23	3
25	2
27	3
40	1
45	1
46	2
48	1
Quadrant Raw Score Total	31

ICON KEY

- Low Registration
- Sensation Seeking
- Sensory Sensitivity
- Sensation Avoiding

Low Threshold (combined quadrant score)

Instructions: Add Sensory Sensitivity and Sensation Avoiding Quadrant Raw Score Totals to get the Low Threshold Raw Score Total

Low Threshold Raw Score Total	23 + 31 = 54

Quadrant Summary

Instructions: Transfer the Quadrant Raw Score Totals from the 7 to 36 months Quadrant Grid to the corresponding Quadrant Raw Score Total box for the appropriate ages. Plot these totals by marking an X in the appropriate classification column (Typical Performance, Probable Difference, Definite Difference)*.

Quadrant	Quadrant Raw Score Total		Less Than Others ← Definite Difference	Less Than Others ← Probable Difference	Typical Performance	→ More Than Others Probable Difference	→ More Than Others Definite Difference
1. Low Registration (7–36 months)	46	/55	**	55	54 --------- X	45 --------- 43	42 --------- 11
2. Sensation Seeking (7–12 months)		/70	70 --------- 44	43 --------- 36	35 --------- 19	18 --------- 14	**
2. Sensation Seeking (13–18 months)		/70	70 --------- 46	45 --------- 38	37 --------- 20	19 --------- 14	**
2. Sensation Seeking (19–24 months)		/70	70 --------- 50	49 --------- 42	41 --------- 25	24 --------- 16	15 --------- 14
2. Sensation Seeking (25–30 months)	38	/70	70 --------- 50	49 --------- 43	42 --X------ 27	26 --------- 19	18 --------- 14
2. Sensation Seeking (31–36 months)		/70	70 --------- 59	58 --------- 49	48 --------- 28	27 --------- 18	17 --------- 14
3. Sensory Sensitivity (7–36 months)	23	/55	**	55 --------- 53	52 --------- 41	40 --------- 36	35 -----X-- 11
4. Sensation Avoiding (7–36 months)	31	/60	**	60 --------- 57	56 --------- 45	44 --------- 39	38 --X----- 12
Low Threshold	**Raw Score Total**		**Note:** This score is only relevant when both Quadrants 3 and 4 are outside the Typical Performance range.				
Low Threshold (7–36 months)	54	/115	**	115 --------- 108	107 --------- 87	86 --------- 77	76 --X----- 23

*Classifications are based on the performance of children without disabilities ($n = 489$).
**There can be no Definite Difference for this section in this age range.

Figure 7.11 ■ **Kaleb's *Summary Score Sheet* (continued)**

Sensory Processing Section Summary (7 to 36 Months)

Instructions: Transfer the Section Raw Score Totals from the 7 to 36 months Caregiver Questionnaire to the corresponding Section Raw Score Total box for the appropriate ages. Plot these totals by marking an X in the appropriate classification column (Typical Performance, Probable Difference, Definite Difference)*.

Sensory Processing Section	Section Raw Score Total	Less Than Others ← Definite Difference	Less Than Others ← Probable Difference	Typical Performance	→ More Than Others Probable Difference	→ More Than Others Definite Difference
A. General Processing	No section raw score total is calculated for the General Processing Section.					
B. Auditory Processing (7–36 months)	31 /50	50 -------- 48	47 ---------- 44	43 ---------- 35	34 ---------- X	30 ---------- 10
C. Visual Processing (7–36 months)	21 /35	35-------- 32	31 ---------- 28	27 ------X- 20	19 ---------- 16	15 ---------- 7
D. Tactile Processing (7–24 months)	/75	75 -------- 68	67 ---------- 62	61 ---------- 48	47 ---------- 42	41 ---------- 15
D. Tactile Processing (25–36 months)	41 /75	75-------- 72	71 ---------- 65	64 ---------- 51	50 ---------- 44	43 X-------- 15
E. Vestibular Processing (7–36 months)	14 /30	30-------- 27	26 ---------- 24	23 ---------- 18	17 ---------- 15	X ---------- 6
F. Oral Sensory Processing (7–12 months)	/35	35-------- 33	32 ---------- 30	29 ---------- 21	20 ---------- 17	16 ---------- 7
F. Oral Sensory Processing (13–18 months)	/35	**	35 ---------- 32	31 ---------- 23	22 ---------- 19	18 ---------- 7
F. Oral Sensory Processing (19–24 months)	/35	**	35 ---------- 33	32 ---------- 24	23 ---------- 20	19 ---------- 7
F. Oral Sensory Processing (25–30 months)	22 /35	**	35 ---------- 33	32 ---------- 25	24 ---------- X	21 ---------- 7
F. Oral Sensory Processing (31–36 months)	/35	**	35 ---------- 34	33 ---------- 25	24 ---------- 21	20 ---------- 7

*Classifications are based on the performance of children without disabilities ($n = 489$)
**There can be no Definite Difference for this section in this age range.

Note: Reproducible Growth Curves for Children 7 to 36 months, for Sensation Seeking, Tactile Processing, and Oral Sensory Processing, are available in Appendix A of the *Infant/Toddler Sensory Profile User's Manual.*

ISBN 076164959-X

PEARSON

Printed in the United States of America.
1 2 3 4 5 6 7 8 9 10 11 12 A B C D E

PsychCorp

Visit www.SensoryProfile.com for additional information and updates.

9 780761 649595

Figure 7.11 ■ **Kaleb's *Summary Score Sheet* (continued)**

When a child has Low Thresholds for responding, that child is likely to be both overly vigilant and rigid, and can respond with irritability at some times and shut down at others. Children with Low Thresholds tend to be fussy and to require a great deal of structure. Therefore, the occupational therapist planned to focus future interventions on defining discriminating sensory input so Kaleb and his family wouldn't feel overwhelmed during daily routines. The therapist also planned to use Kaleb's visual processing strengths to assist with his functional performance in areas of concern.

When discussing his Probable Difference scores in Auditory Processing, his family shared that they don't see how noises interfere with Kaleb's day. The therapist noted that Kaleb seems to notice sounds more that his peers, which may interfere with his concentration. His parents reported that while he tends to be distracted by noises, it doesn't stop him from finishing meals or playing a game.

Intervention

The family decided to focus on expanding Kaleb's dietary range. Kaleb typically refused new foods when his parents introduced them. He even would refuse familiar drinks if not offered in a familiar cup, displaying his need for contextual routine and visual sameness to limit unfamiliar stimuli. His parents had been introducing a few bites of a new food on its own plate, with his preferred food present and available after he finished the new food. The therapist commended the parents for this strategy, explaining that they were helping Kaleb manage the amount of alerting information, so he could slowly increase his repertoire of tolerated foods. In addition, they mainly introduced the request visually (the small amount of food on his plate and the preferred food nearby), which incorporated Kaleb's strengths in Visual Processing.

However, portions of this process were still stressful to Kaleb and his family. Kaleb was as prone to engaging in an outburst as to accepting the new food opportunity. Therefore, the therapist suggested modifying the way his parents introduced a new food. They maintained the structure of the situation and the visual information. The therapist suggested that they try starting with a food Kaleb enjoyed while changing one thing about it. For example, Kaleb preferred noodles, yet would refuse all meats. His mother placed a few small shreds of chicken into the noodles. They matched the color and flavor of the broth with the noodles. The family planned to increase the number of shreds and then the size of the pieces of chicken. Mom suggested that they could change the shapes of the noodles (e.g., flat or round, cut into smaller or longer strips) without changing the flavor. This suggestion indicated that mom was beginning to understand the level of detail they would have to attend to in order for Kaleb to progressively accept a wider range of food choices.

During Kaleb's morning routine he had refused to have his teeth brushed, nails clipped, or take baths. The therapist theorized that this related to his Definite Difference scores in the Low Threshold quadrant and in the Tactile Processing and Vestibular Processing sections. Therefore, they maintained the same approach to structure and offering visual information for Kaleb during these activities. In addition, the therapist shared information about alerting and calming techniques, especially related to touch and movement. For example, when unexpectedly splashed, Kaleb becomes more alert. The therapist related how the water provides a calming touch during bathing as the water presses against Kaleb's skin, and suggested deeper water for bath time to completely cover his legs and hips. Also, Kaleb started out in sitting and then his mother tipped his head back to wash his hair, which is also alerting. His mother decided to try some different positions in the bathtub so she wouldn't have to tip Kaleb's head back so often. They also tried different washcloths and hand placements to offer calming (firm pressure) touch input. The therapist suggested warming the bathroom before bathing Kaleb to reduce the alerting input from temperature differences between the feeling inside and outside the water.

The therapist had noted that Kaleb's mother had marked items in the profile about Kaleb's resistance to cuddling and being held even though mom had not brought up this subject during their conversations. The therapist also observed the stress Kaleb's responses (e.g., pulling away, crying) had on mom, who would recoil when he reacted negatively. In past experience, the therapist had noted some parents seemed uncomfortable broaching this issue, perhaps because of the broad social implications of a child "not liking mom." The therapist wanted to provide strategies for broaching this area of performance without embarrassment. The therapist discussed offering calming touch input while holding Kaleb in the context of bathing (e.g., carrying him while getting supplies, holding him while drying him off). They also discussed the importance of pressing firmly to put lotion on his body, and talked about creating a lotion time for mom and Kaleb to put lotion on together, each doing their own bodies at first, and then introducing shared opportunities (e.g., Kaleb rubbing lotion on mom and vice versa).

Outcomes on Intervention

During the first attempt with the chicken, Kaleb noticed the new food and refused to try it. Mom was delighted that her idea of changing the shape of the pasta without changing the flavor or adding things was the most successful first change to his eating patterns. They put just a few flat noodles in with the round ones, and then kept changing the format a little bit as Kaleb became more adaptable. After two months, the team tried even smaller and fewer pieces of chicken in an attempt to introduce an amount of change that would allow Kaleb to explore new food flavors along with the pasta shapes, and without increasing his stress levels to the point he would refuse. After a few months, Kaleb would eat a bowl of ¼ chicken and the rest noodles. Because Kaleb's refusal of new foods was so pronounced, the family decided to introduce only one new food at a time.

His mother relayed that Kaleb started to smile during bath time. She found that laying him in a reclined position (with support from big foam sponges) decreased Kaleb's resistance to bath time. The therapist pointed out that the sponges provided both postural support and firm touch on his back and that both aspects were helpful for Kaleb. She also found he preferred a bath "puff" to a washcloth; she bought several colors and let Kaleb pick which one they would use. Mom and Kaleb also began a ritual of scrubbing each other with the puffs, which increased their interactions, Kaleb's sensory input, and mom's sense of satisfaction with their bonding.

During a visit to the parents' house, the therapist observed Kaleb's mother holding Kaleb to read a book. Dad reported that he could carry Kaleb like a baby monkey on his back if Kaleb was secured with a tight blanket. Both parents commented that these activities were very satisfying for them, and made the more difficult tantrums easier to handle.

APPENDIX A

Child's name:______________________________ Birth date:______________

Sensation Seeking Growth Chart

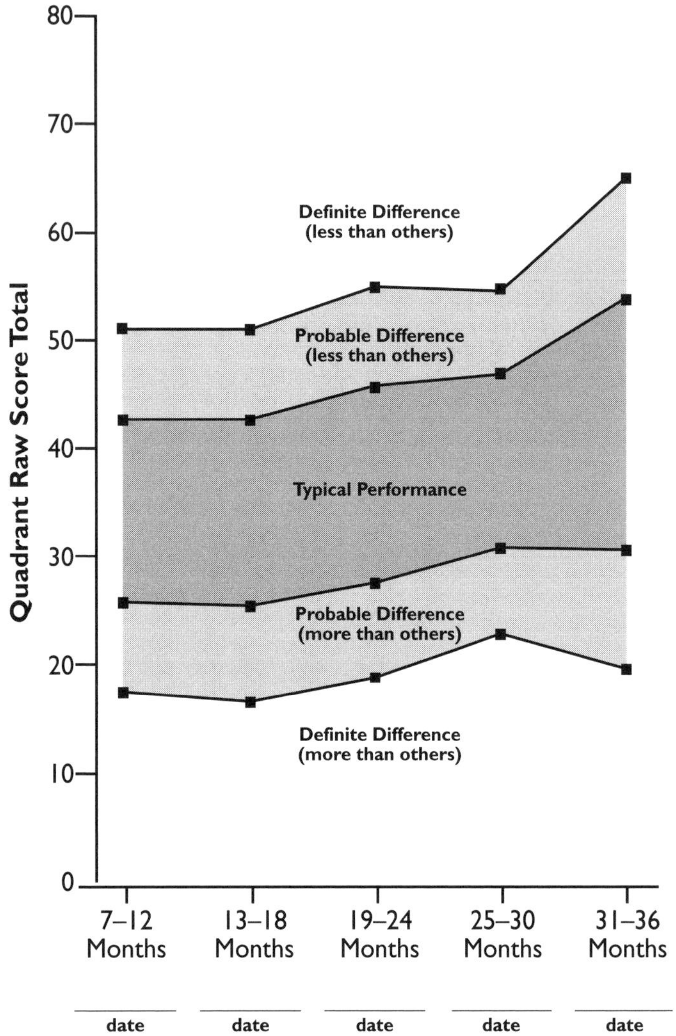

Tactile Processing Growth Chart

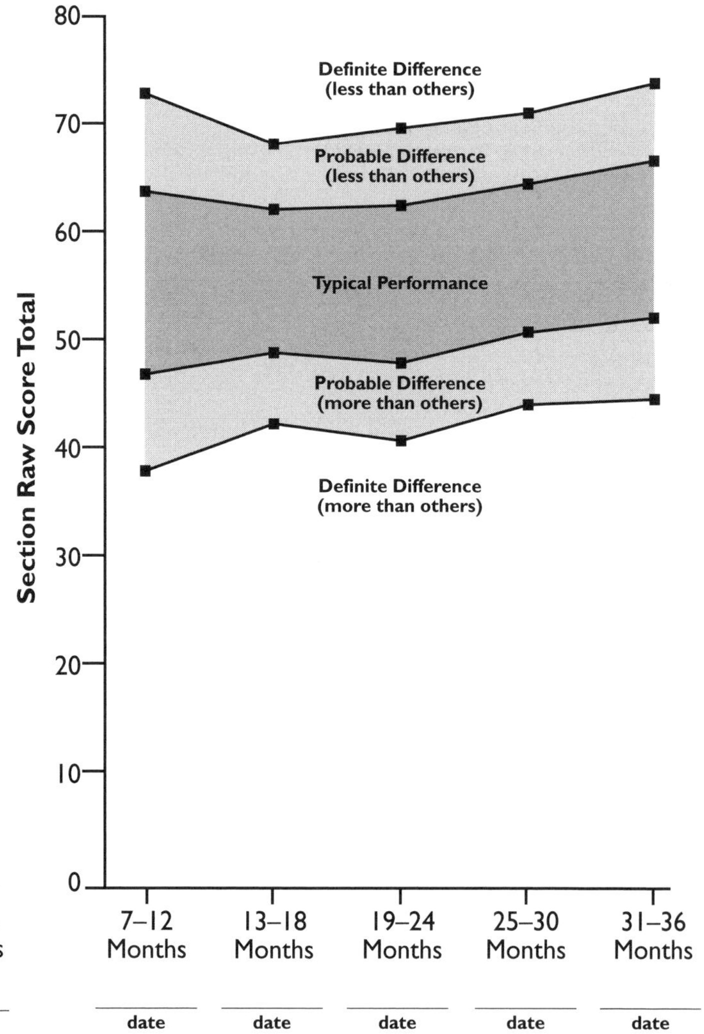

Note: These growth charts represent developmental trends in these particular scores.

Child's name:________________________ Birth date: ______________

Oral Sensory Processing Growth Chart

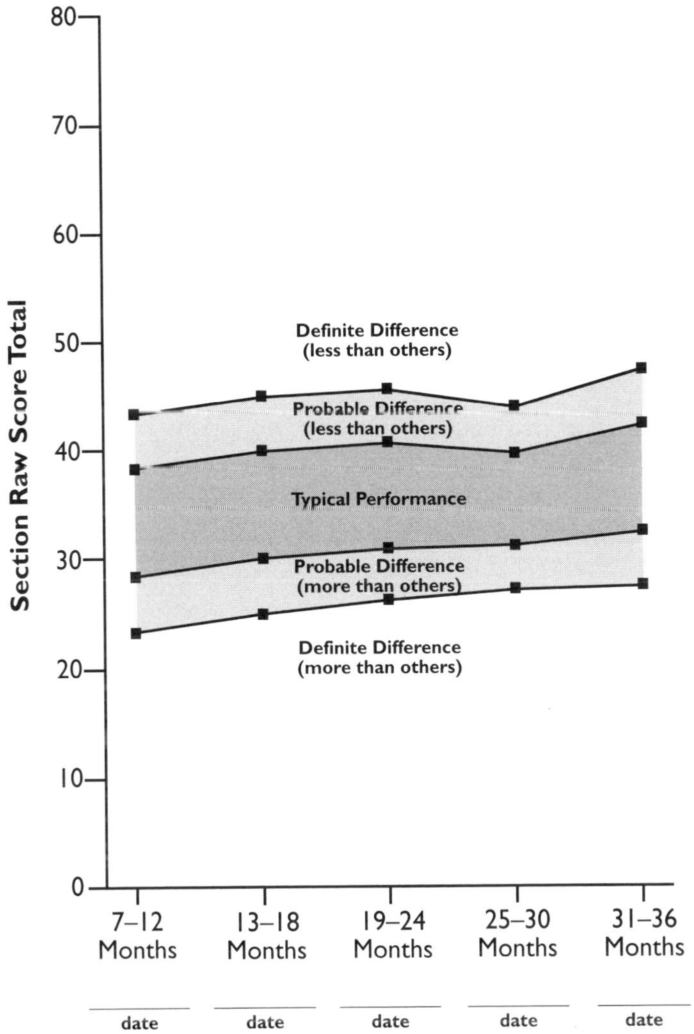

Note: These growth charts represent developmental trends in these particular scores.

APPENDIX B

Comparisons of Means and 1 *SD* Ranges for Children With and Without Disabilities (Ages Birth–6 Months)

Quadrants

Quadrant 1: Low Registration	0 5 10 15 20 25 30 35 40 45 50 55 60 65
Children Without Disabilities (Birth–3 Months)	[----x ----]
Children Without Disabilities (4–6 Months)	[----x----]
Reflux (*n* = 21)	[x]

Quadrant 2: Sensation Seeking	0 5 10 15 20 25 30
Children Without Disabilities (Birth–6 Months)	[---x---]
Reflux (*n* = 21)	[x]

Quadrant 3: Sensory Sensitivity	0 5 10 15 20 25 30 35 40 45 50 55 60
Children Without Disabilities (Birth–6 Months)	[------x------]
Reflux (*n* = 21)	[x]

Quadrant 4: Sensation Avoiding	0 5 10 15 20 25
Children Without Disabilities (Birth–6 Months)	[-x-]
Reflux (*n* = 21)	[x]

Combined Quadrant

Low Threshold	0 5 10 15 20 25 30 35 40 45 50 55 60 65 70 75 80 85
Children Without Disabilities (Birth–6 Months)	[---------x---------]
Reflux (*n* = 21)	[x]

Comparisons of Means and 1 *SD* Ranges for Children With and Without Disabilities (Ages 7–36 Months)

Quadrants

Quadrant 1: Low Registration	0 5 10 15 20 25 30 35 40 45 50 55
Children Without Disabilities (7–36 Months)	[---x---]
Developmental Delays (*n* = 69)	[---------x---------]
Health Impairments and Metabolic Disorders (*n* = 29)	[x]
Pervasive Developmental Disorders (*n* = 24)	[--------x--------]

Quadrant 2: Sensation Seeking	0 5 10 15 20 25 30 35 40 45 50 55 60 65 70
Children Without Disabilities (7–12 Months)	[--------x--------]
Children Without Disabilities (13–18 Months)	[--------x--------]
Children Without Disabilities (19–24 Months)	[-------x-------]
Children Without Disabilities (25–30 Months)	[------x ------]
Children Without Disabilities (31–36 Months)	[----------x ----------]
Developmental Delays (*n* =69)	[-------x -------]
Health Impairments and Metabolic Disorders (*n* = 29)	[x]
Pervasive Developmental Disorders (*n* = 24)	[---------x---------]

Quadrant 3: Sensory Sensitivity	0 5 10 15 20 25 30 35 40 45 50 55
Children Without Disabilities (7–36 Months)	[-----x-----]
Developmental Delays (*n* = 69)	[-------x-------]
Health Impairments and Metabolic Disorders (*n* = 29)	[x]
Pervasive Developmental Disorders (*n* = 24)	[-------x-------]

Quadrant 4: Sensation Avoiding	0 5 10 15 20 25 30 35 40 45 50 55 60
Children Without Disabilities (7–36 Months)	[-----x-----]
Developmental Delays (*n* = 69)	[--------x--------]
Health Impairments and Metabolic Disorders (*n* = 29)	[x]
Pervasive Developmental Disorders (*n* = 24)	[----------x----------]

Combined Quadrant

Low Threshold	0 ... 40 45 50 55 60 65 70 75 80 85 90 95 100 105 110 115
Children Without Disabilities (7–36 Months)	[-----------x-----------]
Developmental Delays (*n* = 69)	[----------------x ----------------]
Health Impairments and Metabolic Disorders (*n* = 29)	[--x--]
Pervasive Developmental Disorders (*n* = 24)	[-----------------x -------------------]

Sections

Sensory Processing

Section A: General Processing

No section raw score total is calculated for this section.

Section B: Auditory Processing

	0 5 10 15 20 25 30 35 40 45 50
Children Without Disabilities (7–36 Months)	[---x---]
Developmental Delays (*n* = 69)	[-------x-------]
Health Impairments and Metabolic Disorders (*n* = 29)	[x]
Pervasive Developmental Disorders (*n* = 24)	[-------x-------]

Section C: Visual Processing

	0 5 10 15 20 25 30 35
Children Without Disabilities (7–36 Months)	[-x --]
Developmental Delays (*n* = 69)	[--x --]
Health Impairments and Metabolic Disorders (*n* = 29)	[x]
Pervasive Developmental Disorders (*n* = 24)	[--x---]

Section D: Tactile Processing

	0 5 10 15 20 25 30 35 40 45 50 55 60 65 70 75
Children Without Disabilities (7–24 Months)	[------x ------]
Children Without Disabilities (25–36 Months)	[------x ------]
Developmental Delays (*n* = 69)	[--------x --------]
Health Impairments and Metabolic Disorders (*n* = 29)	[x]
Pervasive Developmental Disorders (*n* = 24)	[--------x--------]

Section E: Vestibular Processing

	0 5 10 15 20 25 30
Children Without Disabilities (7–36 Months)	[-x-]
Developmental Delays (*n* = 69)	[--x--]
Health Impairments and Metabolic Disorders (*n* = 29)	[x]
Pervasive Developmental Disorders (*n* = 24)	[---x---]

Section F: Oral Sensory Processing

	0 5 10 15 20 25 30 35 40
Children Without Disabilities (7–12 Months)	[---x---]
Children Without Disabilities (13–18 Months)	[---x---]
Children Without Disabilities (19–24 Months)	[---x---]
Children Without Disabilities (25–30 Months)	[--x--]
Children Without Disabilities (31–36 Months)	[---x---]
Developmental Delays (*n* = 69)	[-----x-----]
Health Impairments and Metabolic Disorders (*n* = 29)	[x]
Pervasive Developmental Disorders (*n* = 24)	[-----x-----]

References

American Educational Research Association. (1999). Standards for educational and psychological testing. Washington, DC: American Educational Research Association.

Ayres, A. J. (1975). *Southern California Postrotary Nystagmus Test manual.* Los Angeles: Western Psychological Services.

Ayres, A. J. (1980). *Sensory integration and the child.* Los Angeles: Western Psychological Services.

Ayres, A. J. & Mailloux, Z. (1981). Influence of sensory integration procedures on language development. *American Journal of Occupational Therapy, 35,* 383–390.

Brown, C., Cromwell, R., Filion, D., Dunn, W., & Tollefson, N. (in press). Sensory processing in schizophrenia: Missing and avoiding information. *Schizophrenia Research.*

Brown, C. & Dunn, W. (2002). *Adolescent/Adult Sensory Profile user's manual.* San Antonio: The Psychological Corporation.

Brown, C., Tollefson, N., Dunn, W., Cromwell, R., & Filion, D. (2001). The Adult Sensory Profile: Measuring patterns of sensory processing. *American Journal of Occupational Therapy, 55*(1), 75–82.

Case-Smith, J. & Bryan, T. (1999). The effects of occupational therapy with sensory integration emphasis on preschool-age children with autism. *American Journal of Occupational Therapy, 53*(5), 489–497.

Clarke, A. M. & Clarke, A. D. B. (1976). *Early experience: Myth and evidence.* New York: Free Press.

DeGangi, G.A., Poisson, S., Sickel, R. Z., & Weiner, A. S. (1995). *Infant/Toddler Symptom Checklist.* San Antonio: The Psychological Corporation.

DeGangi, G. A., Sickel, R. Z., Wiener, A. S., & Kaplan, E. P. (1996). Fussy babies: To treat or not to treat? *British Journal of Occupational Therapy, 59*(10), 457–464.

Dunn, W. (1991). The sensorimotor systems: A framework for assessment and intervention. In F. Orelove & D. Sobsey (Eds.), *Educating young children with multiple disabilities: A transdisciplinary approach.* (2nd ed., pp. 35–78). Baltimore: Brookes.

Dunn, W. (1994). Performance of typical young children on the *Sensory Profile*: An item analysis. *American Journal of Occupational Therapy, 48*(11), 967–974.

Dunn, W. (1997a). The impact of sensory processing abilities on the daily lives of young children and their families: A conceptual model. *Infants and Young Children, 9*(4), 23–35.

Dunn, W. (1997b). Implementing neuroscience principles to support habilitation and recovery. In C. Christiansen & C. Baum (Eds.), *Occupational therapy: Enabling function and well being.* (pp. 182–232). Thorofare, NJ: Slack.

Dunn, W. (1999). Assessment of sensorimotor and perceptual development. In E. V. Nuttall, I. Romero, & J. Kalesnik (Eds.), *Assessing and screening preschoolers: Psychological and educational dimensions.* (2nd ed., pp. 240–261). Boston: Allyn & Bacon, Inc.

Dunn, W. (2001). The sensations of everyday life: Empirical, theoretical, and pragmatic considerations, 2001 Eleanor Clarke Slagle Lecture. *American Journal of Occupational Therapy, 55*(6), 608–620.

Dunn, W. & Brown, C. (1997). Factor analysis on the *Sensory Profile* from a national sample of young children without disabilities. *American Journal of Occupational Therapy, 51*(7), 490–495.

Dunn, W., Brown, C., & McGuigan, A. (1994). The ecology of human performance: A framework for considering the effect of context. *American Journal of Occupational Therapy, 48,* 595–607.

Dunn, W. & Daniels, D. (under revision). *Initial development of the* Infant/Toddler Sensory Profile.

Dunn, W., Myles, B., & Orr, S. (2002). Sensory processing issues associated with Asperger's Syndrome: A preliminary investigation. *American Journal of Occupational Therapy* [January/February 2002].

Ermer, J. & Dunn, W. (1998). The *Sensory Profile:* A discriminant analysis of young children with and without disabilities. *American Journal of Occupational Therapy, 52*(4), 283–290.

Fisher, A. G. & Murray, E. A. (1991). Introduction to sensory integration theory. In A. G. Fisher, E. A. Murray, & A. C. Bundy (Eds.), *Sensory integration: Theory and practice.* (pp. 3–26). Philadelphia: F. A. Davis.

Fisher, A. G., Murray, E. A., & Bundy, A. C. (Eds.) (1994). *Sensory integration: Theory and practice.* Philadelphia: F. A. Davis.

Gorsuch, R. (1983). *Factor analysis.* Hillsdale, NJ: Erlbaum.

Kandel, E. (1993). Cellular mechanisms of learning and the biological basis of individuality. In E. Kandel, J. Schwartz, & T. Jessell (Eds.), *The principles of neural science.* (3rd ed., pp. 1,009–1,031). New York: Elsevier.

Kandel, E., Schwartz, J., & Jessell, T. (Eds.) (2000). *The principles of neural science.* (3rd ed.). New York: Elsevier.

Kemmis, B. & Dunn, W. (1996). Collaborative consultation: The efficacy of remedial and compensatory interventions in school contexts. *American Journal of Occupational Therapy, 50*(9), 709–717.

Kientz, M. A. & Dunn, W. (1997). A comparison of the performance of young children with and without autism on the *Sensory Profile. American Journal of Occupational Therapy, 51*(7), 530–537.

Magrun, W. M., McCue, S., Ottenbacher, K., & Keefe, R. (1981). Effects of vestibular stimulation on spontaneous use of verbal language in developmentally delayed young children. *American Journal of Occupational Therapy, 35,* 101–104.

McIntosh, D. N., Miller L. J., Shyu, V., & Dunn, W. (1999). Overview of the *Short Sensory Profile.* In W. Dunn, *Sensory Profile user's manual.* (pp. 59–73). San Antonio: The Psychological Corporation.

Ottenbacher, K., Scoggins, A., & Wayland, J. (1981). The effectiveness of a program of oral sensory-motor therapy with the severely and profoundly developmentally disabled. *Occupational Therapy Journal of Research, 1,* 147–160.

Pohl, P., Dunn, W., & Brown, C. (submitted). *Interacting with sensory information from daily life: The sensory profile of older adults.*

Zero to Three Diagnostic Classification Task Force. (1994). *Diagnostic classification of mental health and developmental disorders of infancy and early childhood.* (S. I. Greenspan & S. Wieder, co-chairs). Washington, DC: National Center for Clinical Infant Programs.